ROUTLEDGE LIBRARY EDITIONS: PSYCHOLOGY OF EDUCATION

Volume 27

UNDERSTANDING CHILDREN

UNDERSTANDING CHILDREN
An Introduction to Psychology for African Teachers

J. S. LAWES AND C. T. EDDY

LONDON AND NEW YORK

First published in 1966 by George Allen & Unwin Ltd

This edition first published in 2018
by Routledge
2 Park Square, Milton Park, Abingdon, Oxon OX14 4RN

and by Routledge
711 Third Avenue, New York, NY 10017

Routledge is an imprint of the Taylor & Francis Group, an informa business

© 1966 George Allen & Unwin Ltd

All rights reserved. No part of this book may be reprinted or reproduced or utilised in any form or by any electronic, mechanical, or other means, now known or hereafter invented, including photocopying and recording, or in any information storage or retrieval system, without permission in writing from the publishers.

Trademark notice: Product or corporate names may be trademarks or registered trademarks, and are used only for identification and explanation without intent to infringe.

British Library Cataloguing in Publication Data
A catalogue record for this book is available from the British Library

ISBN: 978-1-138-24157-2 (Set)
ISBN: 978-1-315-10703-5 (Set) (ebk)
ISBN: 978-0-415-78597-6 (Volume 27) (hbk)
ISBN: 978-1-315-22778-8 (Volume 27) (ebk)

Publisher's Note
The publisher has gone to great lengths to ensure the quality of this reprint but points out that some imperfections in the original copies may be apparent.

Disclaimer
The publisher has made every effort to trace copyright holders and would welcome correspondence from those they have been unable to trace.

Understanding Children

AN INTRODUCTION TO PSYCHOLOGY FOR
AFRICAN TEACHERS

BY

J. S. LAWES
Westminster College of Education

AND

C. T. EDDY
*Westminster College of Education
Formerly Principal Education Officer
(Teacher Training) Ghana*

London
GEORGE ALLEN AND UNWIN LTD
RUSKIN HOUSE · MUSEUM STREET

FIRST PUBLISHED IN 1966

This book is copyright under the Berne Convention. Apart from any fair dealing for the purposes of private study, research, criticism or review, as permitted under the Copyright Act, 1956, no portion may be reproduced by any process without written permission. Enquiries should be addressed to the publishers.

© *George Allen & Unwin Ltd.* 1966

PRINTED IN GREAT BRITAIN
in 10-*point Times Roman type*
BY WILLMER BROTHERS LIMITED
BIRKENHEAD

AUTHORS' PREFACE

Psychology, even that section of it which is relevant to teaching, is a large subject; in this small book we hope to arouse an interest in it on the part of students and teachers, resulting in further study of children, and organized reading. Our aim is threefold. First, and most important, to establish in the reader the attitude of regarding children as individuals, each with his own characteristics and problems, resulting from differences of heredity and environment. Secondly, to provide a background of knowledge, to help in the understanding of pupils' learning and behaviour. Thirdly, to stimulate the teacher to observation, enquiry, and thought, rather than passive acceptance, either of traditional classroom procedures, or of the content of this book.

CONTENTS

1. *Children are Individuals* — 11
2. *What makes Children Individuals?* — 21
3. *How Children Learn* — 33
4. *Learning and Understanding* — 52
5. *Why do Children differ in Attainment?* — 68
6. *Children differ in Behaviour* — 83
7. *Understanding Children* — 94

GLOSSARY OF PSYCHOLOGICAL TERMS — 102

INDEX — 106

CHAPTER 1

Children are Individuals

ALL the school-children in the little town had been given a holiday for the Independence anniversary celebration, and in their smart clean uniforms were marching proudly past the District Commissioner and his guests on the town football field. 'Which is your daughter, Mr Mensah?' asked the new college teacher from Britain; 'They all look alike to me.' 'That's Comfort,' was the reply, 'the tall, thin girl in the third rank, and that is Mr Dako's daughter next to her – the one who walks with a slight limp.'

When a teacher first faces a new class containing pupils whose ages are all very much the same, they often all seem to be alike, as they did to the newly arrived teacher from overseas. As the teacher gets to know them better, they begin to appear less alike, more as differing individuals. Some stand out as individuals sooner than others; this one because he is by far the tallest in the class, that one because he is the shortest; one because he is always the first with his hand up to answer any question, another because he is always the last to finish any piece of work. Then there are those who distinguish themselves by their behaviour, usually by actions intended to attract the teacher's attention. All these we note for being extremes, for being the most: the tallest, the shortest, the most bright, the slowest, the most talkative. There are many others in the class whom we may get to know much more slowly, the ones who are not outstanding one way or another. These we might call average children, but they are just as much individuals as those who impress us more. We all have our individual differences, and vary from one another in many different ways, in many different characteristics.

If we get all the children in a class, all of about the same age, and stand them in a line, we can arrange them from the shortest at one end to the tallest at the other, as in Diagram 1.

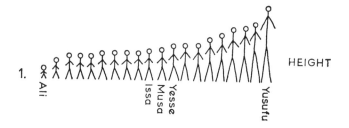

At one end we have the tallest, at the other end the shortest, and around the middle a number who are near average for height. But if we now take the same pupils and again arrange them in a row, this time with the brightest child at one end and the slowest learner at the other, we find that many of them have changed places. Diagram 2 shows the pupils graded in order of ability; Musa, who is average for height, has turned out to be the most able boy, while Yusufu, who is the tallest, is among the middle group, nearer the average for ability.

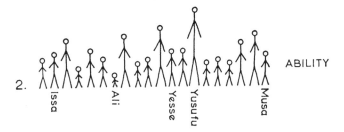

We could line up the same group yet again, say for behaviour, and find that once more there was re-arrangement of position. The third diagram shows that the tallest boy,

CHILDREN ARE INDIVIDUALS

Yusufu, who is about average for ability, is frequently in trouble for behaviour; Musa, who does not show up as either tall or short, but is clever, is also one of the best behaved; Yesse is one of those pupils who are about average in physical size, ability, and behaviour.

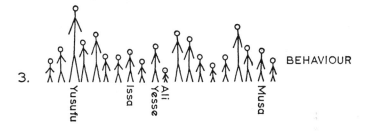

3. BEHAVIOUR

Note that we are not saying that the tallest boy is always the naughtiest, or that the cleverest pupil is always of medium height, but that if any group of people is studied closely they soon emerge as individuals, as Ali, Musa, Yusufu, and so on, because each has his own characteristics, for some of which he is more noticed than for others. Each has a certain height, a certain amount of intelligence, a customary level of behaviour, for example in punctuality, tidiness, helpfulness, and many other characteristics which we have not yet mentioned; what makes each a recognizable individual is the combination of characteristics that is his own.

One of the important things in understanding children is to recognize that there are many sides to each child, and knowledge of just one or two of these does not mean that we know all about the child. For example, because we know that a child has been called 'intelligent' by his teacher, this does not tell us that he will be successful in everything that he attempts, that he will be good at games, for example, that he will always be well behaved in school, that he will later be a good father. To understand children properly, we must think about them in many different ways; this book will describe some of them.

So far, only the members of one class have been considered. Much can indeed be learned from the study of the pupils in one class, from making comparisons, from discovering the features that they have in common and the ways that they differ, and later in this book readers will be encouraged to study their own pupils in detail in this way, but there is a limit to the amount of information that one class alone can provide. It may be that a teacher has a class all of whom are very hardworking or clever, or all of whom are badly behaved; that teacher might get a false picture of what children in general are like. The results of studies made on large numbers of children help to overcome this danger. These studies are of two types. There are studies of the type described above, where children of the same age are compared for a number of factors such as physical features (height, weight, eyesight, etc.); intellectual characteristics (intelligence, ability to learn, skill at languages, etc.); social qualities (friendliness, ability to lead, helpful behaviour, etc.). Investigations like this, carried out on large numbers of children, are called 'cross-sectional' studies, because they look at children from different sections of society, from different schools, for example, or from a number of different tribes, or from both town and country. The second kind of enquiry is concerned with following children through the stages of their growing, rather than comparing different children at one time in their life. These are called 'longitudinal' studies. A longitudinal study of one child will give some information, but this could be misleading, for this particular child might develop abnormally fast, or abnormally slowly; so for this type of study, also, as large a number of children as possible is required.

From these two kinds of enquiry a number of rules or principles of development have been drawn up:
1. Children differ greatly in their rates of development; one may develop rapidly, another much more slowly.
2. A child may vary in its own rate of growth; at some

time during its childhood it may grow rapidly; at others it may be making little progress.
3. Different aspects of growth may proceed at different rates; for example, mental growth may not be as rapid as physical.
4. Despite the different rates of growth, each child passes through the same stages in the same order; for example, each crawls before it walks, speaks before it reads.

It is important that these principles are remembered when reading this book, or other books about children, and when studying real children. You may come across statements such as 'in general children . . . ' or 'the average child can . . . .' These statements are useful guides, but not to be taken as completely true about each and every child. You will certainly come across pupils who do not seem to fit the general patterns described, perhaps because they are in advance of their age, or because they are developing slowly, or even because their behaviour is so unusual that it is difficult to regard it as an individual variation of the general basic pattern. But in the main the statements made, the descriptions given, will help to explain the behaviour of most children.

Causes of difference

What makes children different: different in physical size, in ability, in behaviour, and so on? One possible answer is that they were born different: that some are tall because they were born of tall parents, and were destined to become tall; that others are short because all people in their tribe are short. There are babies who seem to be troublesome and badly behaved right from the time they are born; others who always seem to be happy and contented. One boy may seem to learn rapidly right from the beginning, while another is very slow. We could say that all these differences were there at birth, that they are 'innate'. But there is another possible explanation: the variations could be the result of the way the children have been brought up. A child can be small not because he was destined to be small, but because he was poorly fed during the early years of his life. Or bad behaviour could be the result of the treatment given to the child by older children or adults. A child in your infants class may cry because he has not been fed, or because he is uncomfortable, or somebody has pinched him! A pupil may be slow at learning, not because he has 'no brains', as is said, but because he has been, and is being, badly taught. If these are the reasons, then we could explain the differences not by saying that they are inborn or 'innate', but by saying that they are due to outside or 'environmental' influences, including in the meaning of this phrase the actions and attitudes of other human beings. Studies and investigations have shown that neither of these types of explanation, innate or environmental, is by itself able to account for all the differences between individual children. The two taken together offer the best explanation; that is, that inborn factors develop under the influence of the environment to make human beings different from one another. For example, a child born with the possibility of being tall, inherited from his parents, will in fact grow to a good height if the conditions for growth are right during his childhood, if he gets sufficient food, and does not suffer a serious illness. The child who from birth is mentally bright will remain so, and improve his intelligence, if he is given the opportunities to exercise his mind, and will do well in school provided that he is competently taught.

We can summarize this by saying that, in explaining and trying to understand children, we must take into account three sets of influences, all of which contribute towards making the child an individual person. These three are:

1. innate influences: those which are present at birth;
2. past experiences: things which have happened to the child during his upbringing, and have had a lasting effect upon him;
3. the present environment: the way in which he is now being influenced by the world around him, and particularly by other people.

Observations and theories

In these first few pages, the words study, investigation, enquiry, and explanation have been used. Before going any further it would be as well to try to give clear meanings to these words. Throughout this book we shall try to make statements which are based on facts, not upon opinion. These facts come from observation of the activities of real people, sometimes children, sometimes adults, where observation of adult behaviour casts some light on the behaviour of children. In the same way, some references will be made to observations of animals, where the results of these observations give some assistance in understanding humans. Studies, enquiries, investigations are all forms of observation, all methods of gathering facts. Sometimes the observations are of children in their natural behaviour, at home or at school, sometimes in specially arranged situations. These specially arranged situations we shall call experiments. The observations on animals are often in experimental situations; we rarely use children for experiments, because animals are at times more easily controlled than children, and because it would be wrong to place children intentionally in conditions which might hinder their development. When a sufficiently large number of facts has been gathered, an attempt is made to draw from them a general rule or explanation which seems to cover all these facts. We can call this rule or explanation a 'theory'. For example, suppose a group of children were given three sets of words to learn off by heart, the three sets being as follows:

1. sixteen words – each 'word' being specially made up so that it was new to the children; each, in fact, meaning nothing, being just a nonsense word;
2. sixteen words – each word being one which the children already knew, but the sixteen being entirely separate, not making a sentence;
3. sixteen words – each word being known to the children,

and this time arranged to make a proper interesting sentence.

Suppose the same amount of time was given to learning each set; if almost all the children were more successful with set 3 than set 2, and more successful with set 2 than set 1, these would be facts, obtained by observing children in a particular situation, and noting the results of their activity. We could then go on to suggest a general rule, explanation, or theory, on the basis of these factual observations: the more meaningful the material set to them, the more successful children are in memorizing. Of course, if this experiment was done with only one small group of pupils, the theory might apply only to that group, and not to all children, so to make the explanation more general we should have to repeat the task with many other groups of children; if we got the same results every time, each experiment would add more and more strength to our theory.

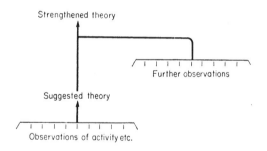

DIAGRAM 4. *The Growth of Psychological Theory*

It is in this way, observation followed by theory, and then checked by more observations, that our knowledge of Psychology – the explanation of human activity, both thinking and behaviour – has been built up over the years.

It sometimes happens that one set of facts can be explained by more than one theory; we shall see this in chapter three, where we try to give explanations of how children learn.

CHILDREN ARE INDIVIDUALS

SUGGESTED EXERCISES, DISCUSSIONS, AND READING

Exercises

1. Make a list of the names of the pupils in a class you know well; at the top of the list place the pupil who is tallest, then the next tallest, and so on down to the shortest member of the class. Put that list on one side, and then write another list, this time putting the most intelligent pupil at the top, and working down to the least intelligent. Make further lists for 'arithmetic skill', 'reading ability', 'regular attendance', 'friendliness', and any other characteristics you may think of. Then place the lists side by side, and compare the positions of individual pupils on the various lists.

    If another teacher knows the same class well, ask him to make similar lists, particularly for items for which there are no mark lists available, (intelligence, good behaviour, friendliness), without his seeing your lists first. Compare the two sets of lists.

2. Make up three sets of words, as explained in this chapter, p. 17, in your own language except for the nonsense words, or use the sets given below. Write each set of words on a large sheet of paper so that all the pupils can see them. Place the first set in front of the class, and tell them to learn the words. At the end of one minute remove the words and tell the pupils to write down all they can remember. When they have finished writing, show them the second list for the same amount of time, and ask them to write down what they remember of that set. Repeat with the third set. Count up the number of words each child has got right on each list. Do they all show the same pattern of results? Can you make a general rule?

    Do the same experiment with other groups of pupils, or if you are a student do it with fellow students. Compare the results from the different groups. Do they strengthen the theory from your first results?

Suggested sets of words:

(The three sets can be used in any order)

noz rij wek hig	cat den bit pot	two men ran off
wuk pef yul vak	jug tip mat net	with my bag and
yos kib jup nem	rag pen fun bat	our dog bit the
faj sab gis mov	tin sad can gun	left leg of one

Discussions

1. What influences, both inborn and from past experience, do the members of the group feel have contributed to their own educational success? Are these influences the same for all members of the group?
2. Consider the childhood history of any man or woman of national or international reputation. Estimate the effect of innate and environmental factors on his career.

Reading. (Books marked with an asterisk * are those suggested for reading by college tutors; the others are for students' reading.)

Hughes, A. G. & E. H. *Learning and Teaching:* Longmans Green and Co. Ch. 4.

Valentine, C. W. *The Normal Child:* Penguin.

*Hyman, Ray. *The Nature of Psychological Enquiry:* Prentice Hall.

*Musson, Paul H. *The Psychological Development of the Child:* Prentice Hall.

Biographies and Biographical novels, such as

Laye, Camara. *The African Child:* Collins, Fontana Books.

Washington, Booker. *Up from Slavery:* Oxford Univ. Press, World's Classics.

Abrahams, Peter. *Tell Freedom:* Allen & Unwin.

Conton, W. F. *The African:* Heinemann.

Abruquah, J. W. *The Catechist:* Allen & Unwin.

CHAPTER 2

What makes Children Individuals?

IN the first chapter we were discussing two distinct themes: development and educational theory: development taking place under the influence of innate factors and of environment, and theory arising from observation and experiment. This chapter will continue the first of those themes and discuss the various factors which seem to influence a child's behaviour. We suggested in an earlier page that there are three groups of factors to consider: innate influences, the effect of past experience, and that of the present environment. These three groups overlap considerably; development and behaviour are the result of the interaction of all three; it is difficult, and indeed unnecessary, to decide on boundaries between them. It is for convenience of discussion that three divisions were set up and are used in the following pages.

Two sets of characteristics which seem very dependent upon inborn factors have already been referred to: physical size and intelligence. To these we would now add temperament or disposition, and certain emotional needs. Through a child's life these may all have some direct influence on how it behaves. Its physical shape, size and strength will allow it to perform, or prevent it from performing, various actions. Its intelligence or mental capacity will have a similar effect on its intellectual performance. Its basic disposition, active or passive, assertive or submissive, may have a general influence on its actions. Those needs which seem to be the underlying influences on human behaviour, such as the need for security and the desire for adventure, will have their effect with varying strength. While all of these, physique, temperament and emotional needs, may have some direct effect on development and behaviour, it is their indirect operation that has the greatest influence.

By indirect operation is meant the way in which these personal characteristics produce reactions in other people and are in turn modified by those reactions. As an example let us imagine a child, physically below average, quiet and rather inactive by temperament, born into a fisherman's family the other members of which are all strong, active, boisterous individuals. It may be that he is accepted as a member of the group, the others being considerate, not expecting him to be so highly active physically, but yet recognizing that he is just as important as a person and has his own contribution to make, perhaps through schooling becoming the business organizer of the family. On the other hand it might be that he is rejected, or expected to take part in all the activities in which the others delight, and yet because of his failure is ridiculed. Starting from the same person, with the same attributes, we can see that the reactions of others can be instrumental in producing two widely varying personalities. The first child may grow up a composed and happy person, the second may try to compensate for his lack of success by petty anti-social activities, or may become lonely and withdrawn.

'What a lovely baby', 'Isn't he an ugly man', 'The first time I saw him I knew he couldn't be trusted', 'She looks so innocent'. We have all heard comments of this sort, the reactions of people to the physical appearance of others. We also know that often the deduction made about character from the appearance is false. There is no particular set of looks which provides the possessor with innocence or honesty. In the same way the possession of looks which could be described as lovely or as ugly is not in itself a guarantee of a particular type of personality. A person of unattractive appearance, or one with a physical deformity, is not bound to be withdrawn, shy and suspicious of other people. If he does become like this it is because people do not like his company, and even greet his approach with looks of horror.

It is interesting to note that the traditional religion of the Yorubas in Nigeria recognized the importance of social acceptance for the disabled. It taught that Obatala, the creator of mankind, fashioned human beings from clay. One day Obatala got drunk, and created albinos, cripples, and blind people, and these are considered to be especially sacred to the god, and given positions of special importance in his worship.

Is the small fellow in the group always aggressive and bouncy? Or is it that some small people develop these characteristics in order to 'hold their own' with other people who otherwise would tend to overlook them? The effect of physique on personality is less a direct one and more an indirect one through social experiences.

One important example of the way in which the influence of other people, in this case the older generation, shapes the life of a child is seen in the different expectations people have of the different sexes. Through the way they are brought up, through the teaching and guidance of parents and grandparents, the differences between boys and girls are widened. After the first few years of life boys are expected to play with other boys, girls with girls; a boy playing in a group of girls risks disapproval or being laughed at. Some playthings are regarded as suitable for boys, others for girls. Boys are encouraged to be energetic and courageous, and to share in swimming, fishing and hunting; the girls are expected to help more with household tasks or with trading, and in some tribes tend to be regarded as inferiors. Weeping is only for girls and women; boys are told to act like men and not to cry, because it is unmanly. In these and many other ways children grow to fulfil expectations. The effect of the group in which the child is reared is of great importance in his development and his behaviour, both during childhood and later in life.

Needs and their Satisfaction

It is held by many people that there are certain fundamental needs of human beings and that the extent to which these are met has a profound effect upon the development of the individual. We are thinking here not so much of needs for food, sleep and warmth, although neglect of these may affect the physical wellbeing and possibly the psychological growth of the person, but of emotional needs such as those we mentioned earlier: the need for security and the need for adventure. Satisfactory emotional development depends upon the satisfaction of these needs.

Emotional security involves a number of factors. It is assisted by a stable and unchanging environment, one in which there is some consistent pattern and routine; for example the child knows that although father is fed first there is a recognized feeding place and adequate food supply for the children. There should be some consistency in what follows what, so that the child knows what will be the consequences of any action, knows too what is acceptable, what will be punished, what will be praised. Such an environment provides a sound framework within which to work, so that energy and thought are not wasted unnecessarily on sheer survival. For children it involves the security of feeling accepted not only by their parents and relatives but also by other children, a feeling of belonging to the group and of receiving affection, approval and admiration from the other members. Security requires the opportunity for giving affection as well as receiving it. Where the people surrounding a child fulfil these requirements by their words and deeds then emotional growth is likely to be normal. The child-raising customs of many African peoples do provide a great deal of affection and protection during the early years of an infant's life. But in all families, African and European, there comes a time of possible difficulty when a new baby appears and takes all the attention. As a child needs to be weaned gradually from its mother's milk to solid foods, so it is better if it is led gradually from receiving the full time attention of an adult to the more independent life of the older child. A sudden change from being the 'baby' to being no longer the central figure in the family may be harmful at the time, and possibly have an effect later in life.

Children seem to have a natural tendency for exploring,

for being inquisitive, for wanting to find out, for collecting objects. This is what the need for adventure includes, and the opportunities for these activities are an important part of growing up. Restrictions of the 'Don't do that', 'Come away from there', 'You mustn't touch that', 'Don't go out of the compound' type, while sometimes necessary for the safety of the child, can have a lasting effect on him so that he becomes afraid to explore, and later in school, when encouraged to find out for himself or to make an individual contribution, he may be too inhibited to do so. The same might be said of mental exploration; if the asking of questions is discouraged by the traditional relationship between child and adult, the natural inquisitiveness may be allowed no outlet, and a brake put on this aspect of mental growth. Exploring with materials in the sense of modelling with clay or carving wood gives opportunities for the exercise of what may be another basic need of the human, the need to be creative. The village child may have better opportunities for this kind of activity; lack of such in towns may lead to this side of the child's inborn ability remaining undeveloped.

The two needs we have discussed here, security and adventure, are linked. The feeling of security is necessary in providing a sound base from which the risks of exploring may be launched; the exploration of the environment, physical, social and intellectual, leads to understanding of it and so enhances the security. One way of looking at the whole process is to picture it as a growth of both an understanding and a feeling in the person that he, or she, is a person in his, or her, own right. One simple example is the collection of all sorts of objects by a child, things which to another person are just a collection of old rubbish, but which to the child mean a great deal because they are his, he owns them. The responsibility for selling the mother's produce, for looking after the animals, for sensible spending of the daily lunch money, contribute to the child's picture of himself as being of some use, of some importance. Gradually the individual grows to take his place as a responsible member of the family and community, an individual with his own life, to be able to make a contribution to the decisions of that community, and to be looked to for these contributions. As the child is given opportunities to undertake responsible tasks and to be of service, in the home and at school, so it is hoped that his development into a responsible adult is encouraged.

Although these developments take place throughout childhood and adolescence it is during this last period, when the youth is attaining physical maturity, that the opportunities for service and responsibility and for the exercise of some individual freedom of choice are most required. Adolescent boys and girls in the modern world, with its extended period of education and dependence, seem more and more to demand their own way, and yet basically they need the continued support and security provided by parents and family as a fixed point from which to venture forth and to which to return if necessary.

Throughout these last few pages we have tried to emphasize the fundamental importance of other people in the development of children. And further than that, that it is the reactions of the other people which are important, reactions which in turn can produce a response, perhaps a permanent attitude, in the child. In one word it is the relationships with other people that have such a great influence during the years of growth. The people with whom the child will have the most significant relationships will be those who are closest to him, in a psychological sense, during the formative years. These people will be those who provide or deny the child satisfaction of his needs, in many cases the mother, probably in a close-knit family the grandmother, at some stage the father, and in some societies other members of the same community.

Effects of experience

In much of what we have said so far the influence of one person on another has been an unconscious one. The older person has not been aware of the effect that his actions may have had on the child. But there are also conscious efforts at influencing the young, attempts at passing on the traditions and attitudes of the tribe and family. This teaching can be through the medium of the spoken word or through imitation by the child of the adult actions. As the influence of the adult or older child is either consciously or unconsciously applied, so the acceptance of that influence by the child can be conscious or unconscious. A lot of behaviour patterns are learnt by watching how another person deals with a situation and then copying his action; if this action is then practised a number of times in that type of situation it becomes a habit, a more or less fixed pattern of behaviour. Thereafter that habit may be used unconsciously whenever an appropriate situation occurs. As well as habits, attitudes of mind may be acquired in the same way, taken over from another person and used a number of times until they become part of the self. Attitudes are fixed opinions which, like the habits of action, come into play in suitable situations and influence the behaviour of the person. For example members of one tribe accept traditional attitudes towards another tribe even where there has been no recent contact. Some tribes are traditionally friends, while others are unfortunately traditional enemies, without reason.

We have so far described habits and attitudes which are consciously acquired even though they may later be used without conscious thought; it is equally possible that habits and attitudes are acquired in the first place without the person being consciously aware of it. Where one person thus consciously or unconsciously models himself on another the process can be described as one of 'identification'. The child acquires the characteristics of another, usually older, person and comes to think, act and feel like that person. The person who is the model is one for whom there is respect, and with whom there is a warm and satisfying relationship. A child will often identify with the parent of the same sex: a boy with his father, a girl with her mother; provided of course that the relationship with the parent is a satisfying one. The parent can help here in two ways; by trying to make the relationship warm and gratifying so that identification will take place, and by being a suitable model so that the right actions, attitudes and sentiments are acquired by the child. If there was but this one identification all children would be close models of their parents. Observation shows us that this is not so, or not so in all cases. In life children will make a number of identifications, with a respected teacher or a series of respected teachers for example, and from each of them gain some influences, so that the eventual personality is a composite of a number of these.

Starting with its inborn characteristics the child through the processes of growing up, and particularly through its experiences with other people, develops its own personal set of behaviour patterns, habits of action, attitudes of mind and emotional sentiments. These will have a decided influence upon the way in which the child will behave in a situation which requires some response from it.

Influences present in the situation

One further group of influences will also be operating; those present in the situation itself. To illustrate this we will look at one or two typical situations in which a child might find himself. James is a bright, active boy, eager to learn and to find out, a boy who has had instilled in him the desire to do well at school and to show a proper respect for his elders. He starts school. There his teacher is a kindly, encouraging man who provides plenty of opportunities for his pupils to explore and to find out things for themselves; he likes them to ask questions and to make suggestions. James soon makes progress in the school, he becomes one of the best pupils, and he often says that there is no other teacher as good as his. James has produced in that situation the sort of behaviour we would probably expect from the short description of him. But let us now suppose that things were different in the school to which he went, that the teacher was one who was afraid of losing control of the class and gave the pupils little opportunity to work on their own, who forbade any talking in the classroom, even the asking of questions, who made all subjects so boring that the class took every opportunity of breaking up the lesson. In this situation we can imagine even James, with his will to succeed and his respectful attitude to authority, joining in with the other boys and breaking the petty rules imposed by the teacher. Sometimes the situation and the fellow pupils in it are stronger influences than personal upbringing. Teachers sometimes meet a mother who expresses amazement that her child is well behaved at school. 'I'm always having to tell him to behave and keep out of my way at home' she says. The teacher does not recognize the description; at school the things to do, the interesting experiences, all appeal to the inquisitive nature which was repressed at home and led to the boy being a 'nuisance'. The same boy in two different situations is behaving quite differently. Then again we may hear of the boy who has always been so well-behaved, so honest and responsible both at home and at school, and yet gets into trouble when with a gang of other boys. In the gang the normal restraints of the home were absent, and in his desire to be recognized as one of the gang, to achieve some self-esteem there, he takes part in some deed of daring which is unfortunately also illegal. We could go on telling stories in illustration; the point is that the situation of the moment is just as much an influence on behaviour as are all the experiences of the child's past. We have tried to summarize the influences, and their interaction in producing behaviour, in the diagram on page 30.

There is one final point which should be noted; those features of the present situation which influence how a child behaves may make a lasting impression; they become in the future part of the past experience. School teachers would do well to remember that the way in which they treat their pupils may be setting up good or bad attitudes towards teachers and school in general, and this will be reflected in their behaviour in other classes and with other teachers.

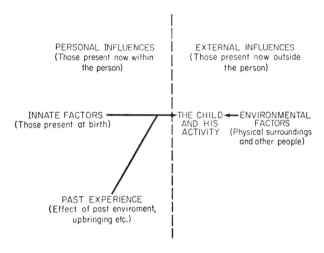

DIAGRAM 5. *Factors influencing a child and his behaviour*

WHAT MAKES CHILDREN INDIVIDUALS?

SUGGESTED EXERCISES, DISCUSSIONS AND READING

Exercises

1. Watch a child in a number of situations. Does he or she show any consistent characteristics, e.g. happy in all situations, nervous in all situations? Or are there some characteristics which vary from situation to situation?
2. Consider the following questions about yourself. How far are you, in your teaching, identifying with one of your own teachers? Are you adopting towards your pupils the attitudes which were those of your teacher towards you and your fellow pupils? Compare your conclusions with those of other students.
3. Have you ever been in a group of friends who propose a course of action which is against your personal wishes? How strong were the pressures to conform? In some other situation would the relative strengths of your personal habits and the group wishes have been different?

Discussions

1. Consider the relative influence of (a) adults other than teachers, (b) school, (c) other children, on the formation of attitudes towards schooling, senior members of the family, the opposite sex, stealing, traditional religious beliefs, physical prowess.
2. To what extent is independence regarded as a desirable quality in your family and community? Or are conformity and co-operation more heavily emphasised? How can the school help the child towards a wise balance in these matters?
3. Discuss what aspects of the organization of the school, and of the teacher's approach to pupils, will contribute to the satisfaction of their need for security and adventure, in the directions outlined in this chapter. Consider this at

both primary and secondary school level; are there any differences?

4. In some African languages the word for 'to educate' means 'to imitate'. Is this significant? What does the word for 'to educate' mean in your own language?

Reading

Fleming, C. M. *The Social Psychology of Education* Chapters IV, V, VI, VIII, IX, X, XI. Routledge & Kegan Paul.

*Mussen, P. *The Psychological Development of the Child* Chapter 5. Prentice Hall.

Sadler, J. E. & Gillett, A. N. *Training for Teaching* Chapter 9. Allen & Unwin.

*Linton, R. *Cultural Basis of Personality:* Routledge & Kegan Paul.

Abrahams, P. *Tell Freedom* Chapter 3. Faber.

CHAPTER 3

How Children Learn

DURING one recreation break, early in his primary school days, Musa sees some boys from a higher class doing forward rolls on the grassy playing-field. He tries one himself, but nearly stands on his head, and topples sideways; he makes a few more attempts, with equally poor results. He watches the others again, and notices that they tuck their heads in very close to the feet; he tries to do this himself, and several more attempts become progressively more successful and less painful. The next day he tries again, and at once produces a much more successful roll, after which he frequently repeats the roll successfully.

Miss Aryee has prepared charts of the multiplication tables for use in her number lessons. On this particular morning she and her class are working on sixes. As she points to a line on her chart, the class read it in chorus. 'One six is six, two sixes are twelve, three sixes are eighteen ...'. After several readings the chart is turned over, and the repetition becomes recitation, still in chorus. The next day the whole table is first repeated; then, for mental work, Miss Aryee fires questions on the table at individuals in the class, and most of them are able to answer correctly.

Miss Ekwensi uses progress charts on the walls of her classroom, to stimulate the children's learning. James is sitting alone, reading and re-reading, and then saying over to himself the poem she has set the children to learn. He wants to see the star on the chart opposite his name that will be the reward for his learning all the four verses. He manages to say them right through to himself, and right through again; up goes his hand; Miss Ekwensi calls him to her desk; he recites the poem correctly, and is given the little star, which he proudly sticks on the chart himself – the first in his class to earn it.

Kofi has completed the ten sums set by his teacher, and puts up his hand to attract attention. The teacher checks them – only seven ticks; 'Do these three again.' Only two of Kofi's friends are left in the classroom now; all the others have been allowed out for recreation. Kofi does not really know what is wrong with his answers, but he rubs them out and tries different ones which may be right. The teacher checks again; two more ticks. A different answer is tried for the last sum; one more tick, and at last Kofi is free.

Mr Mutasa has carefully prepared the apparatus for his arithmetic lesson. He distributes strips of cardboard to the children, who have been arranged in little groups. Each group has a lot of short pieces labelled 'one inch', some bigger pieces marked 'one foot', and a couple of larger ones labelled 'one yard'. The children are told to match the pieces and find out what they can. One groups quickly finds that three one-foot pieces are as long as one yard; another puts twelve one-inch pieces together and makes one foot. Mr Mutasa then gives them lengths of string, and they are asked 'How long is that?' One group finds that it is the same length as fifteen of the one-inch strips; another places beside it one foot and three one-inch strips. One bright boy then suggests that instead of working with the little one-inch pieces they could mark the 'one yard' strip with distances of one inch, and measure any piece of string against that.

All these stories, as you probably realized while reading

them, are descriptions of situations where the process which we call learning was going on. In this chapter some of the ways in which learning might be explained will be examined, but first we need to be clear in our minds what we mean by 'learning'. In a class we may use all sorts of ways to get the pupils to give the answer twenty-four to the sum 4 x 6 and at the end of the lesson we may have persuaded every child to give this answer. The real test of whether they have properly learnt or not comes during the next lesson, when, if we start by giving the same sum, we say of those who can still give the answer that they have learnt, and we are disappointed in the others, who we say have not learnt. Learning, then, consists in dealing with a situation on one occasion and then using this experience when a similar situation occurs later. Not all of the stories above show both these stages; the story of Kofi and the one about Mr Mutasa's class describe only the first situation; the stories should go on longer if they are to illustrate learning or not learning, but in the shorter form they will help us to present the theories with which different psychologists have tried to explain what goes on when someone learns. We cannot see this something which goes on within the child; we only conclude from his later behaviour that an earlier experience has had an effect on him. In the story of the class learning the six times table we decide from the way that they are able to answer questions in the second lesson that the pupils had gained something from the first one. Before the first lesson they did not know the table; during the first lesson something happened which meant that when the second lesson came round they did know the table. The different theories offer us some words, some ideas, which are useful in explaining or understanding what is going on in a child's mind when he is learning.

One theory which is often used describes the learning process as one of forming bonds, of making connections. We cannot see these bonds, but they are a useful explanation. We could say that in learning the six times table the children were forming bonds between, for example, the words 'three sixes' and the word 'eighteen', so that when later the first phrase was said they were able to respond with the sound 'eighteen'. Similar bonds would be formed for each part of the table. Putting it into diagram form, we indicate the bond by a straight line:

three sixes —————— eighteen
four sixes —————— twenty-four   etc.

A general diagram which could be used to explain this and many other examples of learning would be

Stimulus —————— Response
or simply   S —————— R

In our story the class repeated the table over and over again; this helped to fix the connections in their minds. The Stimulus —————— Response theory says that practice strengthens the bond; the more a response is made in a situation the more likely it is that the same response will be used the next time that situation turns up. Have you ever seen a class respond to the stimulus of the bell ringing by closing their books, even though the teacher is still continuing the lesson?

If the connection between a situation and a particular response is going to be strengthened by practice, we must be certain that the response being made is a correct one. Suppose one of the children chanting tables had been saying 'four sixes are twenty-one', over and over again; then it would have strengthened this bond, and would have learnt a wrong response. In the story of Musa learning a forward roll, improvement was made through practice, but not through practice alone; when Musa failed, he looked how others were performing, and tried to correct his errors. He must have known two things: what a successful roll was like, and when he failed to achieve this. As a general rule we might say that practice alone does not make perfect; practice of the right move, or the right answer, helps to make the performance perfect.

Not all of our stories tell of children learning by repetition and practice of one particular response. Kofi kept trying to do his sums, getting different answers each time until he got the ones which the teacher said were right. As soon as he got them right he was released from any further work at them. If learning is explained as bond-formation, how was the bond strengthened in this case? An extension of the Stimulus-Response theory uses the idea of strengthening or 'reinforcing' the bond through the satisfaction of a need present in the person at the time he makes the right response. Kofi had a 'need' to escape from the classroom into the playroom, and the moment he got the sums correct this need was satisfied. We could use the same explanation about James learning the poem; he has a need to be successful, to learn quicker than the other pupils. This need was satisfied when he was awarded the star. Or perhaps we should say that this need was reduced rather than completely satisfied, for it it is likely that we should see the same need arising in James in a later lesson. This theory, then, is one of 'reinforcement of bonds through need-reduction'.

```
KOFI            NEED────────────NEED REDUCED
                'to escape'              by being allowed out
                   SITUATION═════RESPONSE
                'sums to do'             'correct answers'


JAMES           NEED────────────NEED REDUCED
                'to succeed'             by getting star
                   SITUATION═════RESPONSE
                'poem to learn'          'correct recitation'
```

These diagrams show the explanation when the correct response was made; if it had not been made, then the need would not have been reduced, and the learning would not have been reinforced. If James had not recited the poem correctly he would not have got the star; when Kofi got some of his sums wrong he was not allowed out, but had to stay and try them again. In both cases the need would still remain. The next diagram shows the bond reinforced because of need reduction when the correct response is made, but not reinforced when some other, incorrect, response is made.

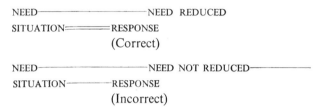

What decides that a response is correct? In the story of Kofi it was the teacher who was the judge, and released the boy when he gave a particular answer; this may have been the only sign to Kofi that he had got the right result. James had two signs of success: the poem in the book, which he could use to check his own recitation, and the star awarded by his teacher. The class of pupils learning the multiplication table also had a model, the table written on the chart, to imitate and to use as a check on their accuracy.

'Understanding' in Learning

We will pause here to comment on these two theories of learning. The main comment we would make is that in describing the learning process as one of making and strengthening bonds, the theories give the impression that all is mechanical; there is no reference to the process which is described in everyday language as 'understanding'. Bonds are formed; how? by imitation, as in the learning by heart of poems and tables; or by repeated trials until the 'correct' answer is hit upon by sheer luck, as in the story of James and the sums. In neither of these instances do we have to introduce the term 'understanding'; the poems and tables could be the imitation of a series of sounds meaning nothing to the child; when the child gets the right answer to the sum he need have no understanding of why it is the right answer; he knows he is right, but not why he is right. These theories are of some use in trying to explain what goes on when a child learns, but before discussing their usefulness we will examine some other theories, in which we find ideas of 'understanding' involved.

It will be useful to describe first some of the animal experiments on which these theories are based. In one type of experiment rats were used, and were required to learn the way through a maze, a series of passages, similar to that in the diagram.

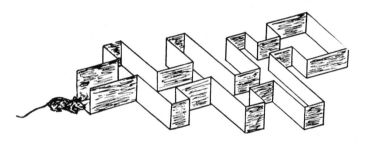

DIAGRAM 6. *Typical Maze for Use in Experiments as Described in the Text*

The rats were hungry, and some of them, when they found the way successfully through the maze, were rewarded with food. These rats, when they were next placed in the maze, ran through quicker, and made fewer mistakes. Each time after that they improved their performance until they ran through without any wrong turnings. We might say, using our previous explanation, that they had learnt because the food they received each time reduced a need, and so strengthened the responses. This need-reduction explanation might also be used for others of the rats who were also put into the maze hungry, but did not find food when they successfully got through the passages. They were not rewarded, their need was not reduced, and it seemed they did not learn, for there was no improvement in their performance, and they continued to make mistakes. But this explanation will not do for a third group of rats, who like the others were put into the maze hungry, and who did not find food for the first ten times that they attempted the task, but who did find food after the tenth on all occasions. During the first ten runs these rats, like those in the second (unrewarded) group, seemed to make no improvement, but after the eleventh run, which was rewarded, they immediately began to run through the maze without any errors at all. The important thing to notice is that they *immediately* performed correctly; they did not start to learn when rewarding began, and then gradually improve, like the first group; they seemed to 'know' already what to do, and proceeded to do it. The explanation which is offered is that while the rats were going through the maze and making mistakes and showing no signs of learning, they were in fact exploring the situation, and mentally learning a sort of map. They were not wandering aimlessly through the maze, but were exploring with some sense of purpose. The results of this purposiveness were only seen by the observers of the experiment when the rats had some reason for producing a correct performance. This type of explanation, that learning is not simply the formation of bonds, but is the result of purposeful exploration, and does not necessarily require reward in the form of need-reduction, is sometimes called the 'Field Cognition' theory, meaning that there is cognition, or understanding, of the 'field', or situation. The situation need not be one in which the 'field' and the mental 'map' built up by the learning are geographical; we could use this type of explanation about the learning done by Mr Mutasa's class, who were exploring the 'field' of measurement in arithmetic, and were building mental pictures of the relationships between the various units of measurement.

Theories of Learning and the Teacher

Here, then, we have three sets of ideas, three theories, to help us in explaining what happens when learning takes place. The three are

(a) Connectionism: learning is the formation of bonds, which are strengthened through exercise;
(b) Reinforcement of bonds because of need-reduction;
(c) Field-cognition; learning through purposive exploration, which leads to the formation of cognitive maps.

All of these theories have something to offer; each of them can be used to explain some learning situations; none of them seem to describe all learning situations. They are best regarded, not as separate theories from which we have to choose one, but as a series with simple connectionism at one end, and field-cognition at the other; in between comes need-reduction, and other theories which we have not mentioned. This series can be regarded as a background scale against which the teacher can place himself as he asks the questions 'Am I teaching this lesson in a way that means I am trying to form bonds in the pupils' minds, regardless of whether they understand or not?' 'Am I making use of the needs present in these children to ensure that they learn?' 'Is this method designed to allow the child to find out for himself, and to reach some sort of understanding of relationships?' If the best explanation of a particular lesson is that it succeeded in forming bonds through continued repetition, it might be useful for the teacher concerned to ask himself the further question 'Could this have been presented in such a way that something more than bonds, some understanding, could have been produced?' On the other hand there may well be some stage in the study of a subject when it is advisable to learn by heart, and to leave the attempt to produce understanding to a later lesson; in which case one theory would provide the explanation of our teaching on the first occasion, and another at the later stage. We do this in drill methods of teaching a foreign language, such as English, by the use of 'substitution tables', which provide many repetitions in rapid succession round the class of the same correct sentence pattern:

This is Comfort's book. It is her book. It is hers.
pen   pen
ruler   ruler

No grammatical explanation, using such terms as 'possessive adjective' or 'possessive pronoun' is given, though this may come much later.

The stories at the beginning of this chapter were chosen so that some, which involved learning by heart or learning a skill, could be explained by one theory, while others could best be explained by another theory. But this means only that one theory had more to offer, the other less, not that one theory alone gave the whole explanation. For example, the table-learning could best be explained as the forming of connections, but there was most probably some understanding, at least by some of the pupils. In this story we place greater emphasis on one end of our series, and less on the other. The emphasis is the other way round in the story of the class doing the measuring: more on the understanding and less on the mechanical end. Not all children necessarily achieved the understanding shown by the brighter ones who made the suggestions; some would learn the relationships by imitating the methods of the other members of their group. This way of looking at learning and teaching in relation to the psychological theories is summarized in the next diagram. In this we have used one more new word in the part referring to the formation of mental maps; this word is 'gestalt' (pronounced

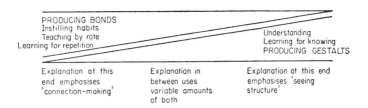

DIAGRAM 7. *Learning Theories form a Series of Explanations. At what Point in this Scale Would Your Teaching be Placed?*

'guess-telt'), meaning a mental pattern or structure which shows the total set of relationships in a situation, in contrast to the series of separate connections of which the theories at the other end of our scale seem to speak.

From these theories, and the experiments on which they are based, we are also able to get a number of practical suggestions for the assistance of the teacher.

Effect of Exercise and Practice

It has already been said that the practice must be of the right response. If we are trying to instil a desired habit, or teach a specific skill, we must make sure that the right habit is being practised, the right moves exercised. For this we must provide the learner with information by giving him a model or example to imitate, and against which he can check his own performance; giving no indication, and leaving the child to try any response until by chance he hits upon the correct one (or gives up in discouragement) is most inefficient. Or we can provide information by arranging that the pupil is told every time that he performs correctly; experiments show that knowledge of results stimulates learning. It is becoming increasingly the accepted practice, for example, for the teacher to go round the class while sums are being worked, ticking correct answers, and putting a finger on errors requiring correction, instead of leaving all marking until books are collected at the end of the period. Thus the pupil gets an early indication of whether he is on the right or wrong lines (and also an early opportunity of further help).

If we want a class to learn by heart, a task which has been given the name of 'rote-learning', and we have only a certain amount of time to allot to this, it is said as a general rule that several shorter periods of practice are more effective than one continuous period. For example, if pupils are to spend one hour learning a poem, three sessions of twenty minutes each would be preferable to one long lesson lasting one hour. It has also been found that if the piece of work to be memorized is not too long, for most pupils it is better to learn it as one whole rather than chop it up into a number of shorter portions. For example, a three verse poem totalling twelve lines would be learnt more quickly if read and recited from beginning to end each time, instead of dealing first with the first verse, then the second when that has been learnt, and then the third. Probably the explanation is that by dealing with wholes the pupil grasps more of the meaning, and it is known that the more meaningful the material, the easier it is to memorize it; also continuous learning establishes the connections between successive lines and successive verses.

It has been found that during the learning of a complex skill, which requires the combination of a number of simpler movements, a person's progress is often not one of continous improvement. Learning to use a typewriter is an example. The beginner, concentrating on hitting the right letters, makes some progress in the speed at which they are found and struck, but soon reaches a maximum speed, and despite further practice does not increase his speed for some time, until one day a further increase in his rate of typing begins. This is shown in the graph; where the line slopes upwards, the number of words typed per minute, i.e. the rate of typing, is improving; where the line is flat, there is no obvious improvement in the learner's speed. As you can see, there are two places in the learning of typing where the pupil seems to be marking time, making little if any progress. The explanation is that at first the learner is typing single letters and not thinking in terms of words; practising the letters he works up to a maximum speed at this, and then makes no more progress; then comes the time when he finds he is striking the group of keys which type whole words, particularly common words like 'the', 'this', and 'that', in one continuous movement, without seeking out individual letters, and practice now improves the speed to a new level. There is then a pause at this speed, until a third improvement comes about, when not just single letters, not whole words, but whole phrases can be typed in one continuous action. The government clerk who is frequently typing letters with the ending 'I beg to remain, Sir, your obedient servant' is able to produce this phrase in one flowing chatter of the typewriter.

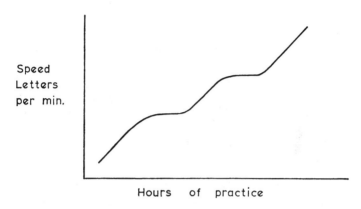

DIAGRAM 8. *Learning Curve – Progress Made in Learning to Type*

We can sometimes see a similar pattern of progress in steps when a child is learning to play a musical instrument, such as a bamboo pipe or a recorder, first playing single isolated notes, then being able to play groups of notes, and finally playing whole tunes through without hesitation. These observations suggest that we should not be unduly critical of a child who, in learning any new skill which requires practice, seems for a time to be making little progress.

Reward and Satisfaction

Rewards are those things which appeal to the needs of the child; in some cases these are tangible things, like sweets, in others they are marks, and in some cases invisible rewards like the satisfaction which success itself brings. There is a tendency for some teachers and schools to think of rewards almost entirely in terms of marks, stars and other tangible objects which pupils seem to appreciate, and to overlook the undoubted value of success and the joy of discovery as being rewarding in themselves. Marks and prizes are incentives set up apart from the work to be done; the situation is one of 'if you do the work correctly then I will give you ten marks'; the interest then lies not so much in the work as in the reward to come. On the other hand if the work is set so that the child has the pleasure of finding out for himself, and so that there is a good chance of success, then no external reward is necessary; the reward is present in, and part of, the study. Whatever form they take, if rewards are to be efficient in reinforcing learning they should be present at the time when the child is successful, or as soon after it as possible; the longer the time lapse between the child making the correct response and receiving the reward, tangible or intangible, the less is the effect of the reward. When a class has completed a piece of work, it should be marked as soon as possible, so that the children get the satisfaction of knowing they are right, and also the reward of the marks, if any, before they have forgotten about the work. Many teachers have noted how soon children come after a school examination to say 'Have you marked it yet?', often before there has been time for the teacher even to have glanced through the paper. As well as being immediate, rewards should be as consistent as possible; ideally every time a child acts correctly he should be rewarded, for if the correct action is not rewarded it is being treated by the teacher in the same way as an incorrect action. In practice, reward is not always possible, but the teacher should try to see that at the beginning of a new piece of learning the pupil gets some reward, if only the reward of knowing that he is right, each time that he is successful.

An interesting new teaching technique pioneered in America which makes use of these two principles of immediate and consistent reward is 'programmed learning'. In this technique the material to be learnt is divided into a large number of very small steps, each of which concludes with something the learner has to do, and each so arranged that the learner is almost certain to be successful in his response. The material is presented one step at a time, either in book form or on a teaching machine; the pupil reads the material, makes the correct response, and moves on to the next step; at the beginning of each new step the correct response to the previous step is given, so that the learner has the immediate satisfaction of knowing that he is right. An example of several steps from a teaching programme is shown in the appendix to this chapter.

The advantages claimed for the teaching machine or programmed textbook are that each pupil can work at his own rate, is almost certain to get each small piece of work correct, and will receive the immediate satisfaction of knowing how well he has done, but the human teacher can learn much about teaching techniques by a study of the principles involved. In routine class teaching the teacher can attempt to order his material in such a way that the pupils are drawn along through the stages, each of which presents little or no difficulty, until at the end they have accomplished a larger advance which, if taken as one stage, would almost certainly present difficulties. Step by step presentation of a lesson, with each step giving some satisfaction to the pupil, does not necessarily mean that the learning is simply 'rote', the establishment of a series of bonds; the steps can be so arranged that the learner is led to some understanding of the topic presented. It is the task of the teacher, with his superior knowledge of the subject, to analyze the topic and break it down into understandable units. The question of what is in fact understandable to children will occupy the next chapter.

SUGGESTED EXERCISES, DISCUSSIONS, AND READING

Exercises

1. Take a subject you studied when at school, and make a list of the topics covered, under two headings: (a) those topics which you think you really understood, and (b) those which you learnt as a series of responses, in order to satisfy the teachers or examiners. Why do you think each of these topics is placed in a particular list? Is it because of the nature of the topic, or because of the teaching, or because of the way in which you tackled the learning, or is there some other reason?
2. Observe a child learning a skill (a) in school, e.g. an arithmetic process; (b) out of school (a child of less than school age), e.g. learning to open a box, or make a simple toy work. Make notes of how the child proceeds. Does he, for example, try lots of different ways until he succeeds, as it seems by chance? Or does he show a purposeful approach? Or after unsuccessful attempts does he ask for a demonstration?
3. Take a topic which would be suitable as the subject for one school lesson period, and break down the material into a series of small steps which seem to you to be likely to lead the pupil to understanding of the topic by the end of the lesson.

Discussions

1. Discuss those rewards, in addition to marks, which the members of the group have seen used in schools. Do you consider that these rewards were successful in getting the children to learn? Were they successful with all children, or were some of them successful with some children only?
2. Each member of the group should draw up a lesson plan on a topic agreed on by the group, and at the group meeting the ideas of the various members can be discussed, and

some decision come to as to which plan seems most likely to be effective; or perhaps the new plan will combine ideas from those of several members.

Reading

Hughes and Hughes. *Learning and Teaching:* Chapters V, IX, XII.
*Peel, E. A.: *Psychological Basis of Education:* Oliver and Boyd.
Niblett, W.: (ed.). *How and Why We Learn:* Faber and Faber.
*Hill, W.: *Learning:* Methuen (University Paper-backs).
Lewis, L. J.. *Days of Learning:* Oxford University Press.
Ghana Teachers' Journal, 1965 No. 1. UNESCO Article on Teaching Machines and Programmed Learning.

APPENDIX

An Example of a Teaching Programme

'Telling the Time'

Read the information in each section, and answer the question at the end of the section. Then move on to the next section, which first gives you the correct answer to the last question, so that you can check your own answer; it then gives you another piece of information, followed by another question for you to answer. Continue in this way through the sections.

(Note that if the programme is in book form, the steps are on different pages, not necessarily arranged in order; at the end of each the reader is told which page to turn to next; on a machine only one section is shown at a time, so that the correct answer does not appear until after the pupil has made his own attempt.)

---

1. On a clock there are two hands, a small hand which points to the hour, and a big hand which tells us how many minutes it is past the hour.
   The hand of the clock which tells us what hour it is is the . . . . hand.

Answer: small

2. The small hand tells us the hour, and is called the *hour* hand.
   The big hand tells us how many minutes past the hour, and is called the . . . . hand.

Answer: minute

3. When the big hand points straight up, the time is 'no minutes' past the hour; that is, it is exactly on the hour. To know which of the hours it is, we have to look at the . . . . hand.

Answer: small, or hour

4. When the big hand is straight up and the small hand is at three it is three o'clock. When the big hand is straight up and the small hand is at eight it is eight o'clock. When the big hand is straight up and the small hand is at five it is . . . .

Answer: five o'clock

5. When the big hand is straight up, and the hour hand is pointing to the figure nine, the time is . . . . o'clock.

Answer: nine

6. At two o'clock the minute hand will be pointing up, straight up, and the little hand pointing to the figure . . . . . . etc.

CHAPTER 4

Learning and Understanding

THE last chapter ended with the suggestion that it is the task of the teacher to arrange his material in order to lead the pupil to some understanding. The way in which this material is conveyed to the pupil is often through the medium of language. In any communication through language it is essential that both the speaker and the listener are using the same language. This is true in teaching, not just in the simple sense that both teacher and child should be using the same national language or local vernacular, but also that the meaning a child attaches to a word should be the same meaning as the adult has for that word. In most teachers' careers there are times when, often to their amusement, a pupil's answer shows a wild misunderstanding that can be traced back to the teacher having used a word in a sense that was completely new and strange to the child. This sort of situation comes to light when the child is putting into his own words what he has learnt; if he is asked to recite the work to the teacher in the exact words that the teacher used there is no check on whether he has understood it or not. We have to distinguish between learning which is purely verbal, the ability to say the words, and learning which involves understanding. Suppose that a lesson had been taught on 'Volume' and that the teacher was testing the class by asking 'What is volume?'. Some answers would almost certainly be 'Volume is length times breadth times height'. Does this show understanding? Or does the pupil who replies 'Volume is the amount of space taken up by an object, and we can measure this by seeing how many cubic inches of space are occupied, by multiplying length by width by height' show much more understanding of all that is involved? Another example could be taken from this book. The reader, in answer to the question 'What is the

Stimulus – Response theory of learning?', might reply 'The formation of bonds which are strengthened through exercise', in the same words as were used in the last chapter; but the authors hope that the reader will be able to put the ideas into his own words, and show that they have been successful in conveying to him the ideas and not just the verbal phrases: in technical language, that there has been learning of 'concepts' not just of 'symbols'.

Concepts and Symbols

Learning symbols is learning to make the appropriate noises of spoken language or the appropriate marks of written language. Learning concepts is understanding what these symbols stand for, what lies behind them. If we were to teach you a new language we could proceed in two ways; we could tell you a word in the new language and then tell you the equivalent word in your own language, thus substituting one symbol for another, or we could arrange for you to have a number of experiences of varied situations in which the new word is used and so let you come to a realization of what the word means, that is, we could help you to form the concept for which this new word is the symbol. Look at the examples in diagram 9; some of these illustrate the word 'kyrnoz'. Are you able to say after looking at these examples what 'kyrnoz' means? If so you have acquired the concept for which 'kyrnoz' is the symbol in this imaginary new language.

Of course we could have taken a short cut and said to you 'Kyrnoz means triangle' and so substituted one symbol for another; this would be perfectly all right if we were already certain that you fully understand the English word 'triangle', that you knew that the word could be used to describe any figure with three sides and not just one particular three-sided figure. (We are certain, of course, that you were aware of this and are simply using it as an example!).

Let us go back to the time when a child first learns the English word triangle. He could learn this by seeing a card

UNDERSTANDING CHILDREN

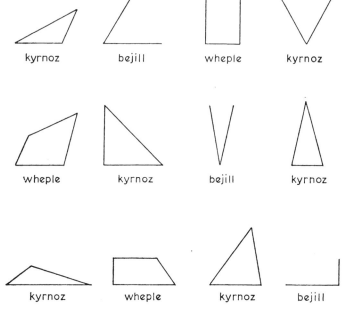

DIAGRAM 9. *For Explanation See Text*

on which was drawn a triangle and also had the word printed on it –

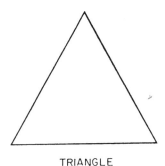

TRIANGLE

DIAGRAM 10. *Triangle*

Seeing this and saying the word a number of times the child would come to 'know' the word, at least in the sense that he associated the word with a figure of that particular shape. But this might be the limit of his knowing. If aided by pictures of other triangles where the sides were of different lengths and the angles varying the child would be more likely to build a more true concept for which 'triangle' was the English label. A concept of this sort is developed from experiences of a number of examples from which a generalized picture of those features which are common to all the examples can be formed. We could define a concept as a generalization which we use when thinking of a particular group of objects. We have, for example, a concept which bears the label 'cat'; this includes all cats, those we have seen and those we have not yet seen but which we will recognise as cats when we do meet them. Similarly for 'bed', 'table', 'book', 'coat', and all those hundreds of common objects which we have come to use, recognize and name in our everyday lives. We should note that the label we use is the one in the language of our own people, but that for others the label will be different although the concept, the generalization behind the word, will be the same. A Frenchman, for example, would use the word 'livre', a German 'buch', a Ghanaian 'nwoma', and yet all would be referring to the same class of objects, the same concept would be behind the differing symbols, the concept we have labelled 'book'. We make this point to underline the theme presented here that the passing from the teacher to the pupil of symbols only is not enough; the symbols are artificial, depending on the society in which we grow up; it is the concepts which are of the greatest importance and which must be passed on to the pupil.

Helping pupils form Concepts

How can concepts be passed on to our pupils? One point we should bear in mind in our teaching is that, as stated above, each of us builds up concepts through experience, and this experience has to be of a wide range of examples. So our teaching should be presentation of as many examples as possible of the idea, the concept, the piece of knowledge we are endeavouring to plant in the pupils' minds. The experience should not be restricted to one of the senses; a lot of spoken descriptions are better than one, but could still leave the child with a concept only partly formed; experiences through other senses, particularly sight but also touch, can help to fill out and complete the concept. In teaching about the structure of plants the whole of the teaching could be through speech, indeed often has been; it would help the pupils' understanding if the spoken information was supplemented by pictures; it would be even better if the class was provided with actual plants to examine and explore. Many a student has 'learnt' from books, from the words, pictures and diagrams presented there, and then later has come face to face with the real thing and found that his mental picture, that is his concept, has not after all been a true one. One of the authors still remembers how as a student he had built up a mental picture of a particular, rather rare, plant and how disappointing it was when some time later he saw for the first time the small miserable-looking real object. English children in Africa, misled by the magnified pictures usually found in Hygiene text-books, have been known to think a daddy-long-legs was a mosquito. And a whole generation of West African standard seven children accepted as accurate, and reproduced in their examination answers, a text-book drawing of a scorpion which, through faulty printing, had one leg missing, though all must have seen a number of real scorpions. The big rule for teaching is to use real material, real situations, reference to the children's own experience for the examples. Real examples and a variety of examples, these will help the formation of concepts.

There will of course be many topics which we have to teach in school in which it is impossible to use real examples, and with these topics it is important that the teacher's understanding of the topic, the teacher's own set of concepts, should be as accurate as possible, and that through his powers of description, use of illustrations, and use of any experiences of the pupils which are similar to the unobtainable examples, he will be successful in getting the children to form accurate concepts. An example would be ice and snow, often mentioned in English literature. Actual ice may now be obtainable from a store or a home refrigerator, but although hail falls occasionally, falling snow is never seen in tropical Africa; its particles can be described as cold, but not hard like hailstones – soft like cotton wool, and falling gently from the sky like the silk cotton drifting down from the tall forest trees in the dry season.

A child organizes his experiences, both those which are part of his everyday life and those which are specially arranged for him by his teacher, into concepts each bearing a word label. This set of concepts helps him to deal with new experiences as they come along. A new object is placed in one of the concept groups and is given the label of that group; if the child can say of a new experience 'this is a cat' or 'this is a teacher', 'that is a book', 'he is an Indian', this helps him to understand the situation and to deal with it appropriately. Note here how useful properly developed language, that is words-with-meanings, is in dealing with life.

All the concepts we have used as illustrations so far have been concepts of objects; to make sense of his experiences and of the world around him a child also needs other, more abstract, concepts. Examples include the concept of 'time', that is an understanding of the meaning of before and after, of how long before and after, of how the units of time such as minute, hour and century are related; the concept of 'cause and effect', that is understanding that there are causes lying outside the child itself. An example of a lack of this concept was seen in the child observed running after a handkerchief blown along the road and who shouted at it to stop. As she shouted the wind dropped and the handkerchief stopped. The girl, who was about three years old, turned to her sister and said 'When I shouted at it, it stopped!' Other concepts are 'space', including the understanding that things are nearer and farther in relation to the child and will also appear differently if viewed from a different perspective; and the concept of 'number'. We will take this last one and use it as an example for what we want to say about all these concepts.

A parent may bring a child to school for the first time and say proudly that little Kofi can already count up to ten. The teacher may suspect that this is just a recitation like saying a poem, and ask Kofi to give him five beans from a boxful. It is likely that when asked to do this several times Kofi may sometimes pick out five, but at other times hand the teacher more or less than this number. Although he is able to use the sound five in its correct place in a recitation of the numbers Kofi is unable to recognize five, recognize a group of five objects that is, not simply recognize the written symbol 5. With any of the concepts the use of words associated with the concept is not in itself a sign that the child has full use of the concept; observation that a child proceeds correctly in a situation requiring the use of the concept is better evidence. When a child recognizes five objects as being five no matter what the objects are, or what sort of pattern they make when placed on the table, then we can be more certain that the concept has been attained by that child.

Because Kofi was unable to recognize five is not a sign that he is lacking in intelligence; many children at the age of school entry, 5 – 6, are at a stage where they are beginning to gain an understanding of numbers and their relationships, but not yet using them correctly in their work. All the concepts we have mentioned, object concepts and the more abstract ones, are not present at birth but are gradually attained during childhood. To adults, using these concepts without really being aware of them, it is difficult to look back and remember early difficulties, but experiments with large numbers of children in a number of countries show that for each concept there is a sequence in its development, with at one age the child not using the concept, then a period during which the concept is developing and when the child will sometimes use it correctly and sometimes not, and then a final stage at which it is fully developed and the child makes use of it correctly whenever it is required. The actual ages will vary a little from child to child, being dependent upon both its innate ability and the richness and relevance of its experiences.

Like the object concepts these concepts are developed through experience; time concepts through experience of situations involving time; space concepts through experiences of situations where exploration of space and the use of the idea of space are required; number concepts through experience of situations demanding the use of number, such as buying oranges or kóla nuts, getting the pencils for the arithmetic group, or playing games like ludo and 'oware' which involve recognizing numbers and counting accurately. Much concept development goes on through the experiences normal to living, growing up, playing and so on; they do not need to be taught like a school subject. The part the teacher can play in the process is to provide experiences and situations, and by watching how individual children deal with situations to decide if they require more and varied experiences to enlarge and enrich their concepts.

Children's thinking

In school the teacher makes use of the knowledge the child already possesses and builds on this to extend the child's knowledge; or, to say the same thing in different language, uses the previous concepts as the basis and endeavours to enlarge these concepts through wider experience and also to introduce new concepts. The teacher hopes that as well as enlarging the child's range of concepts he is also preparing the child to reason for himself. Reasoning, in the sense of taking a problem situation and being able to reach a solution to it, can involve objects like solving a jigsaw or a string puzzle, or deciding how to make something with wood or metal, or it can be entirely a mental exercise with concepts being manipulated in the mind instead of pieces of string or wood with the fingers. In either case what we call thinking is involved. The experiments of a Swiss psychologist Jean Piaget have shown that the thought which a child is capable of is different from that of an adult. We have already given one example of this with the girl and the handkerchief. Unable at her age to grasp ideas of physical causes independent of herself she 'reasoned' by associating two things which by sheer chance happened at the same time, the shouting and the handkerchief stopping; to her one thing must have caused the other. Another example is shown by one of the most famous of Piaget's experiments. A child is shown two equal sized glasses each containing the same depth of an interesting liquid such as Coca-cola and is asked questions, such as which one he would choose, which show that he realizes that they both contain the same amount. Then, as the child watches, the liquid from one of the glasses is poured into another, differently shaped, container and he is again asked to compare them.

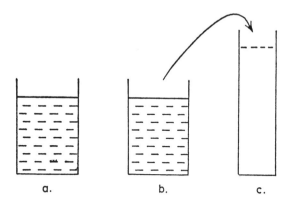

DIAGRAM 11. *Conservation Experiment – for details see text*

Children up to an age of six or seven years will be unable to understand that the amount of liquid has remained the same and will choose one of the vessels as containing more, basing this judgment on the impression that the shape makes. In the picture for example the glass C might be said to contain more because the liquid is higher in it. Older children will be able to make correct judgements, and we can say that they are able to conserve, to understand that the amount stays the same even if the shape alters, and that they are able to reverse their thought, that is to think back to what has gone before and not to make their judgment solely on the present impression.

There seems to be a series of stages that the child passes through, from the time as a very young baby when he is almost incapable of thought up to the time when he is capable of adult logical thought. For the first few years of life the child is in the early stages of concept formation, is beginning to form that mental picture of the way in which the world around him is organized which will go on developing over the years that follow; he will be dealing with the problems of life not by 'thinking' but by associations. He will learn that if he makes a particular sound then he is fed, that when a particular person comes to him comfortable feelings follow, that a certain sound is associated with feelings of discomfort. As language develops and the child is able to remember, to deal with mental representations as well as with direct associations, then some sort of 'thinking' is possible. This early type of thought, represented in the story of the glasses of Coca-cola, has been called 'intuitive' thought, since the child makes use not of logical processes but of intuitions or guesses based upon inadequate impressions; he does not take into consideration all the information. For example the Coca-cola was judged to be more because it came higher up the glass; no note was taken of the fact that the glass was narrower. The child was unable to deal with the notions of taller and narrower at the same time.

After about the age of seven the child is able to think more logically, more in terms of the problem set, using all the information available and not ignoring part of it or being led astray by hasty judgements. He is able to use correctly the concept of conservation, the understanding that things retain their basic properties despite changes in appearance. He will be able to reverse the sequence of his thought operations and go back over the stages of his reasoning, a valuable check when problem-solving. He will be capable of classifying, putting things which are alike in one group and distinguishing them from things which make up other groups. He can arrange them in a line from shortest to longest or the other way round. These processes mean that he can deal with tasks and school subjects which require the operations of classification and of recognizing relationships. The child's thought is now more like that of an adult, except that he can only reason with tangible objects or in terms of tangible objects with which he is familiar. Because of this reliance on real objects this stage has been called the stage of 'concrete' thinking.

The last stage comes in adolescence when the young boy or girl is more and more capable of what is called 'formal' thought, that is reasoning which is no longer tied to tangible material, and which can solve problems by imagining possibilities, and by forming theories and alternative explanations which are then tested mentally against the information given in the original statement of the problem. Perhaps one familiar example of the difference between concrete and formal thought is to be seen in school geometry. Often the earlier stages of this are taught in a concrete way with the pupils abstracting the properties of triangles or parallelograms by examining and measuring a number of examples of each. A favourite task is to establish that the sum of the angles of a triangle is 180 degrees by cutting out paper triangles, tearing off the corners and placing them together. Contrasted to this is the later stage when a formal proof has to be produced with its 'given', 'suppose that', 'therefores', and all the rest of the logical proof.

The ages which have been attached to the three stages described should be looked upon as guides only; one stage gradually develops into the next; nothing magical happens suddenly on the seventh birthday or at any other age. The important

LEARNING AND UNDERSTANDING

thing is the sequence of stages, which seems to be the same for all children; some whom we call more intelligent probably pass through the stages more quickly and attain the formal level earlier, while others develop more slowly, reaching that stage later; some of the slower may never reach the final stage. This is not a tragedy; much of life can be dealt with by thinking of a concrete nature, and even those who are capable of formal thought often return, or regress as we call it, to the lower type of reasoning; when the problem is one which is solvable concretely there is no need to be 'formal'; when the problem is one which is of unfamiliar type to the solver it often helps to put it into concrete terms. Many a secondary school pupil after manipulating x and y and z in a piece of Algebra has finally put numbers in place of the letters to 'see if my answer will work'! There are examples of highly regarded academic persons who faced with a situation outside their own field of study revert to the concrete level or even right back to the intuitive level. There was a professor of philosophy who went to the railway station in his home town to start a journey, forgot where he was travelling to, looked at his ticket, unfortunately at the return half, saw the name of his own town and immediately went home!

What implication has all this for the teacher? We would make just a few suggestions. It has been said that to teach a child a subject it is necessary to know both the child and the subject. In the context of this chapter 'knowing the child' implies observation of each child with the purpose of gathering clues as to the level of concept development and the level of reasoning reached. The use of questioning can be helpful here, questioning which does not require simply the recitation of verbal phrases but attempts to probe the child's understanding. Examples can be found in the exercises at the end of the chapter. Experiments of the type which Piaget himself uses are there suggested; others may be found in some of the books listed. Experiments on these lines will be useful as informal checks on pupils' progress. Having thus gained some idea of each child's position the teacher can try to provide those experiences which may widen the child's range of concepts and strengthen already developing concepts, these experiences being closely linked with the appropriate language. Further than this the teacher can attempt to teach in ways which require reasoning at the pupil's level of thought; thought does not develop without the opportunity for it; lessons which can be learnt by heart will do little to encourage thinking. In the teaching of any subject the teacher might bear in mind Piaget's claim that concrete experience and thought must precede formal thought. In this we can see justification for many of the modern activity methods used in our more progressive schools. There is a need for these beyond the infant level. As well as proceeding from the concrete to the abstract the approach to any topic might be thought of as one of matching the structure of the child's thinking to the structure of the subject. Ask oneself 'Are the thought processes which this topic requires for its real understanding the thought processes which my pupils are capable of at their stage of development and experience?'

One might also ask 'Are there any experiences which I can provide for these pupils in order to assist the development of concepts which seem to be not fully formed?', and 'Can I present this topic in a way which involves the children in thinking at their level of reasoning?'.

This last question raises two points of teaching technique. Involving children in thinking 'at their level of reasoning' can mean simplifying the subject so that, without drastically altering the basic ideas, the child is better able to cope with the concepts involved. But it can mean, particularly with secondary pupils, presenting the work in a way which requires the exercise of more mature reasoning, of 'working it out for oneself' rather than simply memorizing facts presented by the teacher. An example is found in geography lessons when a map is presented showing natural features such as hills, valleys, river and vegetation but bearing no signs of man-made buildings and developments. The pupils are required to reason out from the information given just where human settlements, roads etc. might be sited. Only after reasoning this out do they compare their conclusions with actual maps showing where in fact such developments have taken place. Any differences between the pupils' answers and what actually happened serve as starting points for further discussion.

UNDERSTANDING CHILDREN

SUGGESTED EXERCISES, DISCUSSIONS AND READING

Exercises

1. With children of various ages between four and eight years, carry out the experiment with glasses of liquid as explained in the chapter. Or, prepare some balls of clay or plasticine two of which are obviously of equal size, the others clearly of other sizes. With children of ages between six and ten years (i) ask 'Pick two balls which are the same' (ii) if the child succeeds in picking the two equal sized balls then say 'Give me one' and ask 'Do I have the same amount of clay as you?' (iii) if the child answers correctly roll the child's ball of clay between your hands to make it long and thin and sausage-shaped, and ask 'Who has most now?'*
Note the ages of the children (a) who succeed in realizing that the amount stays the same although the shape alters (i.e. those who are able to 'conserve') and (b) those who do not succeed.
*(Note that the phrase 'who has most' is grammatically incorrect but that it has been found that young children understand this better than the phrase 'who has more'; another example of children's understanding being different from that of the adult).

2. Count out six beans or nuts from a box into a straight row in front of a child. Say to the child, who is provided with a box containing a large number of beans, 'You make a row with the same number in it'. If the child succeeds spread your row wider but do not alter the number of beans. Say to the child 'Make your row the same number'. If the child succeeds push your row into a rough pattern, not a row, and ask the child to make the same number. (Note that the directions say 'Make the same number' not 'Make the same pattern'). Do this with children of various ages and note the ages at which (a) the children copy the pattern but alter the number and (b) keep the number the same even though the pattern alters. These latter children have a more fully developed number concept.

3. When a child gets a wrong answer in, say, an arithmetic sum, instead of simply saying 'That's wrong', take time and ask 'Tell me how you got that answer?'. This may often reveal not a careless error but a genuine misunderstanding by the pupil, who was working correctly within his limited understanding.

Similarly when using oral questioning in any lesson, instead of dismissing an answer as wrong follow up the answer with one or two questions to find out why the child gave the answer.

Does this questioning technique (a) give you some insight into the pupil's understanding, (b) aid the pupil to gain greater insight and understanding?

Discussions

1. In a group discuss how you would set about providing experiences to help children to form the concepts of (a) gas (b) century (c) cubic yard (d) glacier.
2. The task of the teacher is that of providing the experiences and material from which the pupil can learn, not to provide ready-made answers. Discuss this with your fellow students.
3. Suggest examples from other school subjects in which the teacher's method requires from the pupils the use of reasoning, as in the geography lesson described at the end of this chapter.

Reading

Isaacs, N. *The Growth of Understanding in the Young Child. New Light on Children's Ideas of Number.*
Educational Supply Association.

*Peel, E. A. *The Pupil's Thinking:* Oldbourne.

Mussen, P. *The Psychological Development of the Child.* Prentice Hall, Chapter 4.

*Lovell, K. *The Growth of Basic Mathematical & Scientific Concepts in Children:* University of London Press.

CHAPTER 5

Why do Children differ in Attainment?

FOR two chapters we have been discussing theories which are useful in helping us to explain how and why children learn, and in indicating to us how we might set about the task of teaching. Now it is time to take up again a point made in the first chapter about children being individuals, and not always behaving in the way the text-books describe for children in general. We particularly want to examine this topic of individual differences as it is seen in pupils' learning. There is no doubting the fact that children vary considerably in the amount which they gain from attendance at school; it is obvious in every school and in every class. Why do children vary so much in school attainment? There are many reasons, and for any particular pupil there may be more than one reason. This chapter will suggest some of the main reasons at present known.

Maturation

Differences exist when pupils first arrive at school; the foundation on which the teacher is to build varies from child to child. There are differences in maturation, experience, and level of concepts. Maturation, becoming increasingly more mature, is the term used to describe the growth of the child which takes place largely under the influence of internal factors. It has been likened to the growth and ripening of a plant. The plant progresses from seed to seedling, to young plant, to mature plant, to flowering, to the production of fruit, and the ripening of the fruit; this goes on almost inevitably; external conditions may speed or slow it, but plants continue to grow, often in the most unpromising soil and climate; there is an internal influence on the growth, a gradual unfolding of potential. Human growth shows the same sort of effect: maturation, influenced by external conditions, yet proceeding despite them.

The importance of maturation in education lies in the claim that certain levels of maturity are necessary for the attainment of certain skills. A child will, for example, walk when it has reached the appropriate stage in its maturation; before this, its own efforts, and those of well-meaning adults who urge it to take its first steps, will have little success, indeed may even have an adverse effect. Experiments with twins have provided evidence for this claim. In this type of experiment, one of the pair is subjected to attempts to teach it or give it practice in a skill such as climbing, or learning new words, before either twin has shown any indication of acquiring the skill on its own. Attempts are made to speed up the learning of one of the pair, but the other gets no teaching, or even practice at the task. The 'speeding up' attempt may achieve some success, but it is found that some weeks or months later the untrained twin reaches a stage in its development when it readily learns the skill, and proceeds to make more rapid progress than the originally 'speeded up' brother. The attempt to forestall maturation has, in fact, usually had a detrimental effect. On the other hand, depriving a child of what would, in another family or tribe, be regarded as the normal opportunity for practice, does not delay development as much as we should expect. Hopi Indians, in North America, bind their children tightly to a board, carried on their mothers' backs, unbinding them only to clean them; such children do not get the same opportunity to practice reaching, sitting, creeping, walking, that children do who spend their day in freedom on the compound floor. Yet these bound children develop the ability to sit, creep, and walk, just as rapidly as children who are never bound; when the right stage of development has been reached, it takes little practice for a human child to develop these capacities. So with some children starting school; they may have reached school age, but be a little slow in maturing in general, or in specific growths required for particular school subjects. For example the maturing of the eye muscles may not have reached the stage where the eyes can be focussed sufficiently well on a page of print for the child to begin reading. Similarly, a child who is ready for large-scale work with a piece of chalk or a thick pencil may not have acquired the finer muscle control necessary for handling a slate pencil or an ordinary pencil in an attempt to practise handwriting.

The first steps in reading provide us also with an example of the value of pre-school experience. Reading involves recognizing a printed pattern, and making the sound for which the pattern is the symbol. This is aided if the printed word is one which the child already knows and recognizes as a sound, i.e. in its spoken form. If the child has had the opportunity to gather a large spoken vocabulary before learning to read, this is likely to help him in his reading progress. In comparison, a child from a home where the family vocabulary is limited may find progress rather more difficult. Similarly, a child whose first reading is in a language not his home language faces additional difficulties. With other subjects, also, experience outside school can be an advantage; for example the child who has actually handled money in buying and selling is likely to master formal money sums more easily than a child who has no such experience.

Learning readiness

These two ideas, of maturation and previous experience, together form the concept of 'learning readiness'. This idea of readiness, introduced into teaching some years ago, resulted in efforts to discover at what exact ages it was best to start particular school subjects, or topics within a school subject. It was stated, for example, that the child of average intelligence could best start learning to read at the age of six and a half. Such ideas proved to be of limited value, since they were based on one aspect only of the child's development. If we add other aspects which influence whether the child is 'ready' or not, the concept of readiness is still a useful one. Still keeping reading as our example, we can list the following factors upon which reading readiness depends:

Physical maturity – e.g. of the eye muscles and of the speech organs.

Perceptual powers – e.g. the ability to distinguish between letters which look very much the same, like n & m, b & d, and to discriminate between closely similar sounds, such as f and th in English.

Intelligence – e.g. the power to make connections between visual and sound patterns.

Past experience – e.g. the use of spoken words in the home, and in preparatory lessons in school.

Emotional development – e.g. is the child capable of co-operating with the teacher; is he now sufficiently secure in the school situation to have confidence to make the attempt?

Motivation – e.g. does the child want to learn to read?

Such an illustrative list shows how complex is the state of readiness in a child, but behind all this lies the basic concern that a child should not be forced into learning too early, so that he copes by learning habits and tricks which satisfy the teacher for the time being but which later prove a handicap. For example he may learn to make the correct sounds associated with the pictures and the limited number of words in a familiar early reading book, but not learn how to analyse and deal with unfamiliar words met later on. It might be better to provide exercises in the processes on which the skill will later be built; exercises in distinguishing visual patterns perhaps, or a widening of the spoken vocabulary. It is one of the skills of the experienced teacher to judge just when a pupil is ready to get most benefit from his teaching.

In some other subjects we could have added to the above list 'level of concept development'; in history, for example, the concept of time, in science the concept of physical cause and effect, and of course the number concepts in arithmetic.

If we suppose the ideal situation in which the pupils all have the required maturity, experience, and concepts, there still remains the question whether they all have the mental equipment necessary to gain the fullest benefit from the learning situations in which they will be placed. We will discuss three facets of this 'equipment': perceptual strengths, imagery, and intelligence. Since children vary in all these, the methods of the teacher should be equally varied, and some suggestions about this will be made later.

Perception and imagery

Learning is the lasting effect of external influences on the behaviour of a person. The way in which the person is in contact with the external influences is through the sense organs, sight, hearing, touch, taste, and smell; in school education the first two on this list are the most important. Defects in the working of any of the senses will be obvious causes of difficulty, but there are less obvious ways in which the use of the sense organs will affect learning. The use of the sense of sight, for example, involves more than the physical process of light rays entering the eye and stimulating the nerve cells within it, although this is a necessary part; the messages which the stimulated nerve cells pass to the brain have there to be made sense of, the brain has to interpret the message. This whole process, from the reception of light sensations to the interpretation by the brain is called 'visual perception'. There are similar processes of reception and interpretation in sound, or auditory perception, touch or tactile perception, and so on. Perception is a process which in itself is in large part learnt; we learn from experience how to judge, or perceive, the distance from us of objects we see around us; we learn to distinguish between sounds. The importance of this for teachers is that individual children may have come to rely more on one type of perception than on another, so that one child may find it easier to learn through listening, while another learns best through looking, and a third makes about equal use of both types. A child who comes from a village where pictures do not exist may arrive at school unable to gain anything from a visual aid of this kind; he has to start learning at school that things which he knows as real can be represented by lines and colours on a flat piece of paper.

Imagery is closely related to perception. Whereas perception requires the object being perceived to be actually present and stimulating the sense organs, imagery does not require the actual object; it is a mental picture or mental sound. Often, when we remember something, we do so by summoning up a mental image of it, imagining the appearance or the sound or feel of the object or event. As with perception, children vary in the strength of their imagery. Many, particularly in the early years of their lives, may be possessors of almost photographic memories, and be able to 'see' in their minds pages of print which they have earlier read. This ability, which has some obvious advantages, usually fades as the child grows older.

Intelligence

'Intelligence' is a word most of us use, probably when we are referring to a person's mental ability, but can we say exactly what we mean by it? Not exactly, in all probability. Most professional psychologists find it difficult to be definite and exact on this point, but there is general agreement among them that intelligence refers to the general, all-round capability shown by a person in all that he does. A person regarded by others as 'highly intelligent' is expected to do well at all mental activities; someone described as being of low intelligence is not expected to be very active mentally. An intelligent person is one who is able to profit from experience and use experience in dealing with new situations, a person who is able to see connections and relationships, and use this information to make further connections. This intelligence, like other human characteristics, is partly the result of inheritance, handed on by the parents at conception, and partly of environment. Intelligent parents often produce intelligent children, but not always; the processes of heredity are not straightforward. In the same way the children of unintelligent parents are more likely to be of low intelligence than of high; but sometimes the reverse does happen: parents of low intelligence – highly intelligent child; or intelligent parents – unintelligent child. This is all a matter of heredity, but even when he has inherited the possibility of high intelligence a child may not show this in his actual performance, if he is not given, particularly during the years of infancy and childhood, the opportunities for the exercise and development of this potential. Cases are known of children who, when placed in families of seemingly higher intelligence, or in classes of supposedly brighter children, have, through living and working in those circumstances, raised their own intelligence nearer to that of the group. We can say that in speaking of a person's intelligence we mean one of two things: (a) the inborn potential intelligence, which can only be suspected from a person's behaviour, but never actually observed or measured, and (b) the intelligence shown in the way the person performs in everyday life. This observed intelligence of course arises from the first, under the influence of environment and upbringing, but if these are not favourable, the inborn intelligence may never be shown to the full.

Each of us possesses some degree of intelligence, but it is present in different amounts in different individuals; some have high intelligence, some low, and many have in-between, or average, intelligence, in much the same way as we described the distribution of height in the first chapter. In some countries and territories the type of education given to a child is based upon, or guided by, the amount of intelligence shown by the child. Rather than leave the assessment of the child's intelligence to the opinion of teachers, or others who know him, tests of intelligence have been devised, so that each child is measured against the same standard, and in the same conditions.

A typical intelligence test consists of a large number, usually between fifty and one hundred, of small tasks, puzzles, and problems; these are presented to the child according to precise instructions, which set down the words to be used by the examiner, the time allowed, and so on, so that each child faces the test in exactly the same conditions. The items included in the test are there because they have been tried out on a large number of children previously, and have been found of such a nature that children of a particular age can solve them correctly, whereas younger children fail to deal with them. If an item is answered correctly by the majority of six-year-olds, but not by most five-year-olds, then it is an item typical of six-year-olds, and a child who can pass on that item, and a number of others of similar standard, is said to have the intelligence of a six-year-old. This is often stated in the form of 'Mental Age'; a child who deals successfully with the test items typical of a six-year-old is said to have a mental age of six; one who deals with items of ten-year-old level is labelled as having a mental age of ten, and so on. A person's mental age may not be the same as his actual, chronological age – the number of years that have passed since his birth. A seven-year-old child may be found able to pass all the tests up to and including those for a child of nine, that is, he has a mental age of nine, and clearly has an intelligence greater than that of most children of his age. A child of ten who has a mental age of ten is of average intelligence; his ability is that of most children of ten. One whose mental age on these tests is less than his real age is regarded as being below average for intelligence.

One of the most important points mentioned in this brief description of intelligence tests is that they are devised by trying them on a large number of children. This means that when a test is given to a child we are in fact measuring that child against the standards set by the hundreds, perhaps thousands, of other children on whom the test was originally tried. It is essential that where intelligence tests are used they should be ones specifically designed for, and tried out in, the region, country, or society in which they are going to be used.

Tasks which are labelled as typical of eight-year-olds in a test published in Britain or America may be using material outside the experience of an African child of that age. For example, one test requires the recognition and naming of a picture of a horse, an animal unknown in forest regions of Africa; an English child would be in equal difficulty if faced with a picture of a scorpion. Tests should be revised, and standards established afresh, if they are used outside their country of origin.

Where such tests are used to decide what type of education a child should receive, it is because it is known that the Mental Age measurement of a child is a reasonable guide to his future attainment in school: a reasonable guide, but not a complete or perfect guide, since scholastic success depends on other things besides general intelligence. Amongst these are the child's special abilities; in addition to general intelligence many children show evidence of particular aptitudes such as verbal ability, mechanical aptitude, mathematical ability, a gift for music or drawing. As intelligence is the result of both inheritance and upbringing, so probably these special abilities arise from inborn potential, and are encouraged and developed by opportunity and experience.

All that we have written so far about maturation, pre-school experience, perceptual differences, imagery, level of intelligence, and range of special abilities serves to emphasize how in understanding children we have to take into account many facets of each individual. We want now to consider how all of these are of importance to the teacher and to the school.

We cannot over-emphasize how important it is not only to know that children differ, but also to know the actual individual children with whom we are dealing; we should discover all we can about the child's previous experience and upbringing; we should note how he stands with regard to the rest of the class in general ability; as he gets older we can try to distinguish those subjects, or groups of subjects, for which he shows aptitude above that of his fellows. By comparison we might also make some decision as to the maturity of the child;

does he seem generally younger than the others, for example? Through inspection of his work we can sometimes decide whether the combination of experience and maturation present is sufficient for the child to achieve understanding of his school work.

Knowing our pupils we can then plan our courses and teaching methods to enable them to make the most of their schooling. A child whose experience before coming to school has been limited can be helped to fill the gaps in that experience. If, as we suggested, some children learn better through the sense of sight, while others find they remember more of what is presented orally, teaching should make use of both channels. The more ways a subject is presented, the greater is the chance that the attention of all the pupils will be held, with each of them gaining something from the teaching. At the same time those who tend to rely on one type of perception and imagery may be getting practice in learning through the other senses. When a class contains pupils whose intelligence ranges from well above average to below average, the work should likewise range across several levels of difficulty, so that each pupil or group of pupils works at a level suited to its stage of development. As special aptitudes develop, particularly during the secondary years, the curriculum might well be arranged so that the choice of subjects can be matched to the particular strengths of the pupils.

Motivation

Even when all these things are noted about each child, and variations and modifications of method and curriculum are made, it is still not possible to say 'All these pupils will now be successful in school'. There is a further, and important, factor influencing how children respond to teaching—motivation.

Children come to school equipped with drives, needs, and attitudes which will influence their reaction to learning and teaching situations. Some drives such as that to explore purposively may be inborn; the need to succeed and do better than others is probably the result of upbringing; other needs and attitudes may be formed during school life; all will have their effect. It is the task of the teacher to make use of, to harness, the motives present in the pupils. If, as is often the case in modern society, competition is a strong motive in most individuals, this can be used to promote learning. If the explorative drive is strong, the presentation of the lesson can allow for the exercise of this.

But this sort of comment is still referring to teaching technique in the sense of how to present the material; beyond all this lies the need to recognize that the school is a social situation, where the pupil is in constant contact with other people, and these contacts have an important influence. The relationship between pupil and teacher is of obvious importance. Both the attitude of teacher toward pupil and that of pupil toward teacher operate here. When the teacher's attitude is one of encouragement and friendliness, includes a sense of humour, and recognizes that pupils are persons in their own right; when he allows discussion, and encourages individual and group activity, and shows himself to be the leader but not the dictator within the group, then the work done by the class is better, and the pupils are contented and friendly. When the attitude of the teacher is an authoritarian one, demanding unquestioning acceptance of orders and instructions, with no attempt to explain reasons or discuss objectives, the work is likely to be of a lower order, the pupils unco-operative, submissive perhaps, or showing aggression towards one another, if not towards the teacher.

The last clause above suggests that the attitude of the pupil towards the teacher is a reaction to the teacher's attitude; this is partly true, but there are other influences shaping the pupil's attitude. The child's home upbringing will have left it with some attitude towards authority: perhaps one of co-operation, or of passive submission, of even of open aggression; this attitude to authority may well be expressed towards the teacher. In some cases there will be specific attitudes towards school and teachers resulting from the attitudes shown by parents or older brothers and sisters, both desirable attitudes and undesirable. We must not forget that as the child progresses through the school his reaction to previous teachers may also have some lasting effect upon his present attitude; his past success or failure will influence his attitude towards particular subjects, and perhaps towards the teachers of those subjects.

It is not only the contact and relationship with teachers which influences a child. His position as a member of a group of pupils is also of significance. Individuals tend to adopt the standards of the group of which they happen to be members. A class, sometimes a whole school, comes to have a tradition of non-success, and this is transmitted to new members of the group. On the other hand a child whose attainment is lower than his abilities suggest that it could and should be is often helped to improve by being placed in a class which is producing better work.

The very fact of working in a group instead of as individuals can have a desirable effect on pupils. Investigations have shown that where pupils have co-operated in work in groups formed by their own choice of workmates, the standards of work have risen, and there has also been improvement in the attitude of pupils towards the subject so studied.

The whole complex pattern of relationships in a classroom has to be taken into account when trying to explain children's performance; the teacher-individual pupil relationship; that between pupils forming the group; and that between the teacher and the class as a whole: a class often conforms to the expectations expressed or hinted at by those in charge of it – a class labelled as 'C' stream has been known to say 'We can't be expected to do that work; we are only 3C'. An individual child in a class may be torn between several conflicting loyalties; she may wish to do well in order to please a teacher whom she admires, yet at the same time have to yield to the pull of the stronger loyalty to the class, which (for example in a class of adolescent girls, looking forward to marriage) thinks little of scholastic success. On the other hand, a boy or girl whose personal inclination is not to conform to the wishes of the teacher may be persuaded to do so because of the disapproval of the class, the desire to stand well with the group being in this case the stronger influence. Although the first part of this chapter made much of the individual variations of pupils, and how these should be recognized and catered for, we have now seen that it is equally important to recognize that the individual is one of a group within which strong social forces will be operating.

WHY DO CHILDREN DIFFER IN ATTAINMENT?

SUGGESTED EXERCISES, DISCUSSIONS AND READING

Exercises

1. Are there any pairs of twins in your family, school or college? Are they identical twins, i.e. of the same sex and identical in physical characteristics? If so, do they differ in achievement and behaviour? Can you offer any explanation?
2. Observe children in the first year or two of their lives. Compare sitting, creeping, and walking ages (in months and weeks) for children who spend most of the day on the mother's back and others brought up European fashion in baby carriages and playpens.
3. If you can obtain an intelligence test, examine the material it contains carefully. In what ways would it be suitable or unsuitable for village Africans? If you can try it on pupils, do so from the point of view of finding out the suitability of the material, not of labelling the children.

Discussions

1. Think of the teacher in whose subject or in whose class you were most successful in your learning. What sort of a person was he? Was he popular with the pupils, a strict disciplinarian, an expert in his subject, did he encourage pupils to learn for themselves, did he forbid talking in class or allow discussion, etc., etc.? Compare your conclusions with those of other students and try to reach a group description of 'the perfect teacher'.
2. How do you set about (a) learning a poem (b) solving an arithmetic problem? Do you, for example, draw a diagram of the problem or copy out the poem; do you make greater use of the sound of the words or of the visual pattern of the words on the page, or imagine the scene of the poem; do you make more progress working alone or in a group, either discussing the problem or simply being together but

working individually; do you give up when you meet difficulty and return to the work later or stick at it until you have finished? Discuss these points and any others which occur to you about learning and compare the ways in which you and your friends differ in learning.

Reading

Fleming, C. M. *The Social Psychology of Education*. Routledge & Kegan Paul. Chapters XIV & XV.
Vernon, P. E. *Intelligence and Attainment Tests*. University of London Press. Chapters 2*, 3 and 9*.
Wall, W. D., Schonell, F. J. & Olson, W. C. *Failure in School:* UNESCO Institute for Education, Hamburg.
*MacArthur, R. S., Irvine, S. H. & Brimble, A. R. *The Northern Rhodesia Mental Ability Survey*. Part I. Rhodes-Livingstone Institute, Lusaka.

CHAPTER 6

Children differ in Behaviour

JUST as children show variation one from another in their school achievement, so variety is seen, though to a less extent, in their general behaviour. We have discussed in chapter two why it is that humans are of such different personalities, why they behave so differently. We saw the effects of differences of inherited temperament, but more particularly the influence of upbringing; we noted how children develop to fulfil expectations, how the group in which they are brought up has an influence on how they will satisfy their needs, and how they will behave in particular situations. We can say that much of a person's behaviour is 'culturally determined', that is, the individual learns particular behaviour patterns which fit the society and conditions in which he is living, and these patterns are the ones which that society regards as satisfactory. When a teacher describes a pupil as 'well behaved', he means that the pupil is acting in a way which he, the teacher, regards as suitable. It is likely that the majority of other teachers would agree as to what is suitable, for they will have come to teaching through very similar school and college careers; thus the teachers' own ideas as to what is good behaviour have been culturally determined, and they are passing on these standards to their pupils. We are all, pupils in their schools, teachers in their classrooms, workers in the fields or factories, wives in the markets, expected to behave in more or less the accepted ways. We say 'more or less', because small differences from the general pattern are usually tolerated; they do not arouse comment or objection; they are individual characteristics which make people just different enough to be interesting. It is wide variatons from the general pattern which are looked upon as wrong, or labelled as bad. Over much of Africa it is considered very bad manners to pass anything to anybody with the left hand. There are probably sound reasons of hygiene behind the custom, but Africans have learnt to tolerate the (to them) peculiar ways of Europeans in this matter; for example, the scouts' left handshake, or at the school distribution of prizes the handing of the prize, and accepting of it, with the left hand, because the right is needed for shaking hands. Other Europeans, in close contact with Africans for a long period, have found they have themselves absorbed the habit of offering things with only the right hand. To be a good member of our society, whether it be school, village, farm, or nation, we are expected to show a high degree of conformity, to behave in the acceptable ways, to have 'adjusted' our actions to the demands of that society.

Adjustment

This term 'adjustment' is useful to us in describing or explaining a person's behaviour. We judge the individual as adjusted when he behaves in the 'right' way, in the way accepted by the group, when he conforms to the general pattern of society. A person described as 'not adjusted' or 'maladjusted' would be one whose behaviour varied so much from the general accepted pattern that he did not fit in, was not acceptable to the group. Given this meaning, adjustment to the society in which the individual is operating, it follows that a person's behaviour might be regarded as adjusted on some occasions, when in one group, and yet be maladjusted when with another group. The schoolboy whose behaviour is adjusted to his gang of fellows, and who is regarded as one of the leaders by them, may, with the same type of behaviour be regarded by his teachers as one of the ringleaders of misbehaviour in class, and as maladjusted to some degree. The normal standards of behaviour accepted by the two groups are widely different. The 'normal standards of behaviour' are sometimes referred to as 'norms' of behaviour. We say that the norms vary from society to society, and that the person is adjusted to the norms of a particular group, and maladjusted when compared with the norms of another group.

As well as having norms which are appropriate to particular societies, we have norms of behaviour which are appropriate to particular ages. We can, therefore, describe a person as adjusted or maladjusted in comparison with the behaviour accepted as suitable to his age-group. Whereas it may be quite natural and normal for a child of four or five to indulge in tantrums and fits of temper and tears, we should regard such behaviour as abnormal in a fourteen or fifteen year old. Thumb-sucking is discouraged in Africa by various devices, and would be regarded as abnormal if practised by a primary school child. Our term 'adjusted', then, refers to a child whose behaviour is regarded by others as suitable for the society of which he is a member, and also as suitable for his age.

How do children become adjusted? By learning the right behaviour patterns. Where do they learn these patterns? In all the situations in which they find themselves, home, village, school, etc. From whom do they learn? From all the other individuals making up those groups. The simplest explanation, and with young children this may well be complete explanation, is that specific responses are learnt for specific situations: when the bell rings, to stop running around and line up near the school entrance; when a visitor enters the classroom, to stand and respond to his greeting; when a bag or handkerchief or other piece of unclaimed property is found in the school, to hand it to the teacher. These responses are learnt because if they are made the child is rewarded by the approval of the school; if they are not made, the disapproval of the school is shown. When teachers speak of discipline in school, they often mean this sort of learning of, and conforming to, rules which preserve the order and peace of the classroom and the school. In order to achieve such a state it is desirable to be consistent and unvarying in the application of approval and disapproval, so that pupils get a clear idea of what kinds of behaviour are acceptable. A child who has learnt the whole range of behaviour suited to the many school situations, and consistently uses those actions, would fit our definition of adjustment: his behaviour would be that expected and accepted by the school society.

But while teachers might regard this external conformity to the rules as being the sign of a well-behaved pupil, they would probably also consider it part of their professional task to help their pupils to judge for themselves what is right or wrong behaviour. Using our terms from chapter four we could express this as 'forming concepts of right and wrong', or possibly we might use the phrase 'moral concepts'. If we wish to instil moral concepts in our pupils, to give them principles to guide their behaviour in school and in later life, it seems reasonable to suggest that these concepts are best developed by the methods previously suggested for object concepts, that is, generalization from a range of experiences which are examples of that concept. To develop a concept of 'honesty' in a child it is not sufficient to talk about what honesty is and how the child should behave; he should have had experience of situations in which honesty is practised, is seen in action; from specific examples the abstract idea of honesty may be built up. It is not what the teacher says which matters, but what the teacher is. One who is frequently late, or obviously neglectful of his duties, cannot train others to give a fair day's work for a fair day's wage. And not only is the teacher important; there are many others whose behaviour is observed and copied by the children. From examples in the life of the school, the child's life out of school, the stories which are read and told in school in history or English lessons, the teacher has opportunities to indicate behaviour which is honest, or just, or kind, or which gives examples of any of those other abstract concepts we hope the pupils will achieve. It is in the period of adolescence that such concepts are often developed. For the pupil remaining at school through the secondary stage the teacher is still an important influence; for those who have gone out into the world other youths and the adults with whom they come into close contact will be of greater influence, but the earlier years in school will in both cases have laid some of the foundations.

We might therefore explain a child's behaviour in one of two ways: (a) it is well-behaved, or adjusted, because it has learnt the right habits for each possible situation, or (b) it is well-behaved because it has developed concepts and principles of behaviour, and these enable it to decide upon the right course of action to take. On the same lines we might explain 'bad' behaviour in terms (a) of having learnt the wrong habits, or no habits, or (b) of not having established guiding principles or concepts. Such explanations, though neat and simple, are not enough to describe all influences on behaviour. In chapter two we wrote about children's behaviour being influenced by the attitudes and sentiments which it develops through its experiences. A pupil may normally conform to a well-ingrained habit of politeness when a visitor comes to the school, but on the occasion when that visitor proves to be a much hated guardian, who has come to the school to take him away, the sentiment may overcome the habit, and the boy disappear from the rows of polite children. Or the child who, through an unfortunate experience or several experiences, has acquired a fear of thunderstorms, may lose for the duration of the storm his usual habit of calm concentration on school work. Hates and fears, loves and joys, can interfere with normal, accepted behaviour. The elder sister who lines up quietly with her class because that is the accepted habit, or because she has understood that this is the most efficient way of getting a number of pupils through a narrow door, may break from the lines, and so break the rules, when she sees her younger sister standing weeping in the confusion of the first day at school.

Ideas of the Self

As well as these attitudes towards things, or situations, or other people or types of people, the child through his life, and particularly through the way other people treat him, comes to form an attitude or sentiment towards himself. If the treatment of other people towards him is such as suggests that they regard him as a clever boy, a boy who is likely to succeed in life, a boy who is popular, that boy is likely to come to regard himself in such terms. If through life the boy has been led to believe that he is inferior, that he is unacceptable as a companion, that the school regards him as unteachable, then he may in time come to have this same picture of himself. It has often been observed by teachers that if a class is regarded as a 'bad' class in work or behaviour, and the pupils are constantly made aware of this attitude, they come to believe it themselves, and to behave accordingly.

'I am as good as anyone in this class; I'll show that I can do the work'; 'I am not liked by any of the teachers; why should I do what they say?'; the child's self-picture can influence his behaviour.

In addition his past experiences will be an influence, perhaps more unconsciously, through the workings of his conscience. We speak of not doing something 'because my conscience would not let me', or after doing something we say 'I was troubled by my conscience'. What is a conscience? Where does it come from? A simplified version of a widely held explanation would be as follows. In the early days and years of a child's life its activities are to a large extent regulated by other and older people, particularly the parents. They show by words and deeds that there are some actions of which they strongly disapprove, and this prevention or disapproval acts as a deterrent to the child, stops him doing what he might wish to do. As the child grows older, these prohibitions are taken into, and become part of, the child's unconscious mind, and in future he refrains from those acts, not because an outside authority says 'Don't', but because this conscience says 'Don't'.

Our explanation of a child's behaviour thus has to take into account a number of influencing factors: innate drives, specific learnt habits, concepts of right and wrong, attitudes, self-regarding sentiment, conscience. All these may be at work within one child, and the resulting behaviour has to conform to the standards demanded by society, if the child is to be regarded as adjusted. The complexity of this task suggests that we should look again at our definition of what adjustment is. As we have so far used it, the term adjustment has referred to a visible conformity to the accepted standards of behaviour. Now we have to add an invisible, personal adjustment of the various influences within the person. The adjusted person is one in whom these various influences have been integrated, that is to say combined to produce a harmonious set of motives which results in behaviour acceptable to the persons around him, and yet is also able to modify his behaviour as he moves from one group of companions to another. This is obviously an ideal situation, and few people would fit this description in every aspect of their life. Children, particularly, are still developing, still learning how to satisfy or control their needs and desires, still forming their self-pictures, still learning habits and principles of behaviour. At some times in their lives they will be able to strike a balance; at others there will be an upset because of a change in the internal influences or the external environment. When the pupil first comes to school there is a big change in all that is going on around him; he has gradually to adjust to these new surroundings. This takes time, and at first he may react to his confusion by temper tantrums, or by being aggressive. Aggression is in many of us a reaction to frustration, to being obstructed in what we want to do; aggression against the frustrating object or person, or when this is impossible, for example when the frustrating person is a teacher, who insists with all the backing of authority on correct work or behaviour, aggression against some other, quite innocent, object or person. In those cases when a teacher finds that punishment of a misbehaving pupil does not result in the desired improvement, it may be that the punishment has merely increased the frustration, and hence the aggressive attitude. Aggression is not the only way in which conflict between opposing motives, or between motives and social requirements, is solved, or worked out. The adolescent girl who desires to leave school and take her place as a grown woman may react to enforced schooling by 'withdrawing' from the situation; though still physically in school she becomes apathetic about school work, or spends the time day-dreaming. Another pupil may react to a situation which makes excessive demands on him by regressing to behaviour which, while suitable for a younger child, is regarded as babyish when indulged in by an adolescent.

For the teacher, the meaning of all this is that not all the children whom we commonly describe as naughty are wilfully behaving badly; sometimes, perhaps more often than we suspect, the child is dealing with the situation as well as he is able. Punishment is not always the best treatment; it may increase the difficulties. If we regard the child as having to integrate and adjust to a number of influences, then we have to recognize that there will be times when the whole balance of that child's life may be upset.

The time of adolescence is one of the occasions in life when the possibilities of upset in adjustment are greatest. There are changes in the internal impulses and needs, such as a strengthening of the sex drive, and a greater desire for freedom from adult control. These changes mean that a new balance has to be struck between the personal impulses and the requirements of the environment. Yet at the same time the environment may be changing. For some it will be a change to the secondary school, where their position will still be that of pupils, this being perhaps in conflict with their hopes of adult status. It may be that they are given more adult responsibility at home and so have two parts to play, a child in school, a man outside. Or it may be that both school and home still treat them as children although they may mix out of school with others of their age who have left school and taken jobs, and so have the greater freedom that wage-earning brings. The physical and emotional changes of adolescence, together with the likelihood of there being more than one set of standards to which they are expected to conform, contribute to the possibilities of adolescence difficulties. Teachers and parents who recognize the difficulties which face these young people can help them to come to a new balance and a re-adjustment.

Starting at school, changing from one school to another, a change at home, with the loss of a mother or father, demands and pressures about work and examinations, are other occasions when the child may be at a loss to know how to cope, and his work and behaviour may suffer. We said at the beginning of this chapter that small differences from the accepted patterns of behaviour are usually tolerated; this is a further plea that pupils should be understood as individuals, each with his task of growing into a responsible adult. Understanding and sympathetic teachers can help in this process; each minor misdemeanour should not be regarded as a major crime; certainly should not be taken as a sign of maladjustment. The term 'maladjusted' is best reserved for the small number of individuals who find it impossible to fit into society, whether it be school or the wider world, and who need the special assistance of experts.

Conforming and not Conforming

Having urged tolerance of individual variations in behaviour rather than insistence on rigid conformity, and pleaded for sympathetic help in some cases rather than punishment, we would finally question whether the demands for conformity are quite so necessary as is sometimes claimed. We are not doubting that certain standards of behaviour are necessary for the life of a school; in any society there must be rules which are for the benefit of all, and are necessary if the society is to function efficiently. We are now questioning the type of education which caters for, and encourages, the conforming individual, and has little time, and no opportunity, for the non-conforming child. Recent work in the United States suggests that teachers prefer the pupil who is a conformist, not only conforming in his behaviour but also in his school work; the child who accepts what the teacher says, who always gives the right answer in the sense of the conventional answer, the one the teacher was expecting, who gets a high score in an intelligence test because this depends upon selecting the answer that the majority of others have selected, who has ambitions which are conventional, who chooses a career of the type usually expected of a person of his ability and education, who writes conventional stories in his composition lessons. In short, a pupil who is, to use the American term, 'convergent', in that he conforms to what is expected. The opposite type of pupil is the one who so often is regarded as a nuisance; the one who asks the awkward questions, and does not accept the conventional explanation; who writes stories which break away from the expected theme; who sees humour in situations where others see none; who may not do so well on the traditional type of examination or in an intelligence test, because he can see other answers than the expected ones, (and if given the opportunity could support them with reasons). These are the 'divergent' pupils, whose thoughts are 'spread out' rather than conforming. The significant thing is that investigations have shown that, given the opportunity, these divergent pupils are as capable of high standards of work as are their more conventional fellow-pupils. It seems likely that the non-conforming, divergent types are those who can make the original contributions to knowledge and to society; their ability to see unusual connections or unexpected methods may produce the advances which are necessary for progress. Without new ideas and innovations society becomes stagnant. We are concerned because many present school methods and systems cater for the convergent pupil; the divergent and possibly more creative pupil is neglected; yet this type of ability is needed in every country and requires encouragement if it is to flourish.

CHILDREN DIFFER IN BEHAVIOUR

SUGGESTED EXERCISES, DISCUSSIONS AND READING

Exercises

1. Make a list of the activities you would consider misbehaviour in school. Can the list be divided into those which are breaking school rules and those which are more serious anti-social actions? What might be the causes of the various misdemeanours? How would you try to deal with pupils who offended in these ways? Compare your lists and comments with those of others.
2. Suggest well-known books and stories which describe behaviour which illustrates the moral concepts we wish to clarify for our pupils.

Discussions

1. 'Every child is in certain respects (a) like all children, (b) like some other children, (c) like no other child.' Discuss this statement.
2. In the light of what has been said in this chapter what can the primary school teacher do to assist the moral development of his pupils?

Reading

Sprott, W. J. H. *Social Psychology:* Methuen, Chapter IX.
Hadfield, J. A. *Childhood and Adolescence:* Penguin.
*Lazarus, R. *Personality and Adjustment.* Prentice Hall.

CHAPTER 7

Understanding Children

IN the previous chapters we have touched on a number of the topics which make up the subject of psychology and which seem to us to have something to offer to the teacher. We have written of needs and potentialities, of maturation, of motivation, of conditioning and concepts, of habits and attitudes, of social adjustment, and of individual differences; all these and many other words, and their associated concepts, we have introduced. How can all this assist in the understanding of children? Basically in two ways we believe. Firstly we hope to have made the student aware of some of the problems of understanding children, and at the same time given him a framework of concepts, together with a vocabulary, which will enable him to systematize his own observations. Secondly, we have tried to draw attention to results from wider observations than any single individual can hope to make, which when added to one's own observations illuminate and enhance them; and we have indicated in our reading lists sources of information about many more such observations.

As an example of the first point let us consider the content of chapters three and four. There we presented a number of ideas about how children learn; two of these are summed up in the two words 'conditioning' and 'concepts'. These are symbols for two different sets of ideas which have been found useful by many people in trying to understand, and to explain to others, how it is that children learn. As the student read those chapters he faced, perhaps for the first time, the necessity of explaining learning, and the possibility that there may be more than one way in which a child learns. After reading and discussing them he realizes the full meaning of the terms, and finds them useful in thinking and talking about teaching and learning in the classroom situation. For example, he begins to ask himself such questions as those suggested in the chapters: 'Am I merely trying to condition these pupils to perform in a particular way?', 'Are these children forming true concepts?'

The second purpose proposed above can, perhaps, be illustrated by reference to the ideas of Piaget, in chapter four, on the sequence of events observed in the development of reasoning in the child. With Piaget's suggested framework before us we can make our own observations of children and compare these observations not only with his, which were on a limited number of children, but also with those of observers elsewhere whose work is becoming increasingly available in books such as those listed at the end of that chapter.

We can refer once again to something we have already written to make our next point. Understanding, we have said, is best brought about by experience of the thing which is being studied, and not by reference to books and other second hand sources; these are aids only. If we wish to understand children we must study children; this is to us the most important message we want to convey. What we have written, the concepts and vocabulary we have offered, are to assist this study; they are not a substitute for it.

Anyone studying children has to be aware of, and to guard against, one particular danger; that of making pronouncements about children in general on the basis of observations of a single child or of a very few children. The authors in their work have met students who preface their remarks with statements such as 'My daughter was able to do that at six years old', or 'My young brother doesn't behave like that', and then, on the basis of this single instance, go on to cast doubt on the results of long years of careful study by many well-known workers and authors. It is to avoid this type of error that child study makes use of what we have called, in chapter six, norms of development or behaviour. Large scale investigations have shown the types of behaviour which are typical of particular age groups of children; the description of intelligence testing in chapter five explained how a child can be described in terms of a mental age by finding out the tasks he is able to perform successfully in a scale of such tasks arranged according to the ages at which the average child can do them. When such age norms are known for development of intelligence, for social behaviour, for the development of skills such as walking or speaking, it assists our understanding of an individual child if we consider our observations against these age-norms. It helps us to understand a child, and to help the child, if we know in which aspects of development he is about average, in which above average, and in which, if any, he is below the expected level. In a country such as the United States, where child study has been undertaken in a highly organized manner for many years, norms for most aspects of development are available to assist teachers who deal with children. In a developing country, where such studies are in an early stage, the teacher has to fall back on his own resources and, while being aware of the limits of his own observations, has to consider the individual children against his own accumulated observations of children of similar ages over the years.

Lest our use of the terms 'about average' and 'below the expected level' in the last paragraph should be read as having an element of condemnation in them for the child about whom they might be used we hasten to add that it has been one of our themes throughout that each child has his own unique inherited potentialities and has been moulded by a wide variety of influences throughout his development, and is thus as different from other children as they are from each other. These individual differences are perfectly natural and the averages or norms are used as convenient guides; to be described as above, at, or below average is a description only and not meant as a judgement of good or bad. We started this book with a consideration of what is meant by average, and showed that although a child may be average for one characteristic we may find him well above or below that mark on others. To make a judgement about a person on one aspect only is as dangerous as to make a statement about all children on the basis of observations of one child only. To say of a nine-year-old child 'he has a mental age of seven' and to dismiss him from any further consideration is both foolish and inhuman. Mental age refers to one rather narrow aspect of the child, his ability to do an intelligence test and other work which requires similar ability. It does not give an indication of his character, his skill as a worker in other fields than those requiring mental reasoning, his ability at getting on with other people or his physical strength. To truly understand a child we need to consider the whole person and not just a limited part of the personality. The word 'personality' in its fullest sense refers to this whole person, to the integration of all aspects – intellectual, physical, emotional and social – which contribute to the human make-up. It is all too easy for the teacher to become pre-occupied with the intellectual development of his pupils and to overlook the rest of the person. The separation of the intellect can be carried to the point where the teacher can speak of the child as having ability but not producing the level of work indicated by that ability because of 'some defect in his personality'; the redeeming feature of such a statement is that although the teacher is speaking as though his only care was the mental development of the child he is showing by his reference to personality that he is aware of other aspects. But the separation of one aspect for attention and the neglect of others should be avoided as much as possible. We have in this book offended in this way by selecting particular features to deal with in different chapters; this has been done deliberately for convenience of discussion, but we hope that the present chapter is remedying this matter by emphasizing the real indivisibility of the human personality. At the end of the last chapter we introduced the term 'divergent' as a description of a type of pupil. This term could be used about the intellectual processes of those pupils, about their emotional state, about their social behaviour; it was in fact used about all of these in the sense that it was used as a description of the whole person, not of one feature in isolation.

Each feature contributes to the personality as a whole and is itself affected by the personality as a whole.

The need to consider the various aspects of a child's make-up as being interlocking and integrated is further emphasized when we deal with pupils experiencing some difficulty in their school work. In many cases we find not only poor standards of attainment but also an emotional state which is operating against scholastic progress. In such a situation we might well ask whether the emotional condition is causing the backwardness or the backwardness causing the emotional state. In all probability the influence is operating in both directions simultaneously, and it is impractical to take either the backwardness or the emotional upset out of context and treat it in isolation; by dealing with one we are dealing with the other. With all pupils, not only those experiencing difficulty, the teacher is influencing the emotional and social development as well as the intellectual growth, whether he is consciously aware of this or not. Since, this is so he should try to be aware of it, and to this end we have included chapters on social and emotional influences on children. These chapters have attempted to consider the child in a wider context than that of the schoolroom, for the concept of the 'whole child' must regard him not as an individual in isolation but as an individual within a particular society. To understand a child we must have some knowledge of the many environmental forces which have acted upon him and are acting upon him; the school is only one of these factors, and although on a calculation of time spent in school it might be regarded as a minority influence we should not allow this to persuade us that, as teachers, we are concerned only with teaching reading, writing and arithmetic; we must never forget that we are teaching children.

SUGGESTED EXERCISES, DISCUSSIONS AND READING

1. Make a careful study of one child whom you know well and have known for some time. Below is a list of some of the points you might note; other points of interest will occur to you as you collect the information. Some of the details suggested are factual, e.g., age, school attended, and will be easily obtainable; others, such as skills, attainments and abilities, while being recognizable, will be of greater value if the child is compared with other children of the same age (e.g. 'his skill at carving wood is exceptional for a boy of seven'); yet other observations involve the judgement of the person making the study and may be influenced by the attitude of that person or his relationship to the child; for example we suggested in one of the exercises at the end of chapter one that you should rate a class of pupils for characteristics such as 'good behaviour' and 'friendliness' and then compare your ratings with those of another teacher; probably you did not agree with the opinion of that other person about every child, for any opinion is partly a reflection of the person making the assessment.

Some aspects for study:

Physical: general physique and appearance, height, weight etc.; general health and serious illnesses which may have had a lasting effect; physical skills, crafts, games played etc.

Intellectual: school attainment, best subjects, worst subjects, general ability relative to other children in class, special aptitudes, interests.

Social: attitude towards other children, parents, teachers etc., the attitude of these towards the child, part played by child in life of the family and the school, qualities such as leadership and organization of other children.

Emotional: expression of emotions, e.g. how often are the following shown: anger, fear, jealousy, pleasure, anxiety;

what seem to be the situations which cause these emotions to be shown?

Background: the home, economic level; standard of education of the parents; customs of the home; size of family, numbers of brothers and sisters and ages of these; changes of home, e.g. from village to town, work done for home and village or responsibilities undertaken by child; schools attended.

2. Make detailed written observations of the activities undertaken by a child or group of children for short periods of time. For example note down all that happens for fifteen minutes then on another occasion make similar observations for another fifteen minutes. On some occasions watch one child, on other occasions watch two playing together, at other times observe the activities of a larger group. Do this with children of various ages. Compare your notes with those of others.

3. Many schools and teachers find it useful to keep written records showing for each pupil such things as background information; progress in school; examination results; abilities; aptitudes and interests; and perhaps character.

Useful points to discuss about record keeping are:

What can the information be used for?

How often should records, of for example progress or character, be filled in?

Who should make the assessments, classteacher or headteacher?

Is there a danger that a new teacher looking at previous records might be influenced by another teacher's comments?

Reading about *record cards:*

Fleming, C. M. *Cumulative Records:* University of London Press.

Peel, E. A. *The Psychological Basis of Education.* Oliver & Boyd. Chapter XVI.

UNDERSTANDING CHILDREN

The following book gives many extracts from *studies of children* in Ghana:

Barrington Kaye. *Bringing up Children in Ghana:* Allen & Unwin.

GLOSSARY

(The meaning required in the text is the one given; there may be other meanings, perhaps more common ones, suitable and necessary in other contexts.)

adjusted: an *adjusted* person is one whose behaviour is acceptable to his companions, and within whom there is no serious conflict.

aggression: a term for feelings of anger or hostility, or the expression of these feelings.

assertive: an *assertive* person is one who tends to make himself prominent, to take the foremost place. (cf. submissive).

attainment: standard or level reached in any activity (used particularly of school work).

attitude: a fixed (but not necessarily unchangeable) opinion which influences a person's thought and behaviour with regard to particular people, objects, or situations.

auditory: concerned with or involved in hearing (cf. tactile, visual).

cognition: a term covering all forms of knowing and understanding.

concept: an idea or generalization which represents a class of things or events, based on the properties they have in common.

concrete: concerned with direct experience with real, actual, specific things, (cf. formal, intuitive).

conserve: a child is said to be able to *conserve* when it can retain the idea of a basic property in spite of changing appearances.

consistent: unchanging

convergent: a term used to describe a person's behaviour or thought if it is similar to that of most others. (cf. divergent).

GLOSSARY OF PSYCHOLOGICAL TERMS

cross-sectional: a *cross-sectional* study is one comparing many children at the same age or stage. (cf. longitudinal).

culture: the customs, habits, traditions, attitudes, beliefs, that are characteristic of a community or a social group.

discriminate: to recognize differences, to distinguish.

disposition: a person's general emotional tendencies.

divergent: differing from most others in behaviour and thought. (cf. convergent).

environment: anything affecting the person but outside him, including other people as well as physical conditions.

factor: an influence which combines with others to produce a result, e.g. inborn and environmental factors influencing the development of a child.

formal: conforming to a pattern or set of rules; formal thinking is the logical thinking of the older child (cf. concrete, intuitive).

frustration: the obstructing or prevention of the carrying out of a desire or intention; or the feeling produced by this prevention.

gestalt: a mental pattern or structure which organizes information instead of attending to its separate parts.

heredity: the passing on from parents to children of physical and mental characteristics; these hereditary characteristics are therefore present at birth.

identification: the process by which a person, probably unconsciously, takes on the behaviour and characteristics of another person much admired or loved.

image: a representation in the mind of something not at the time making any impression through the senses.

Imagery is the ability to summon up such images, or the process of doing so.

innate: present at birth.

integrated: combined to produce a balanced whole; an *integrated* person is one in whom there is no serious conflict of internal motives.

intelligence: in a general sense, the all-round ability shown by a person in his life and work.

intuitive: a term applied to the reaching of conclusions without making conscious use of all the facts, partly reasoning, partly guessing. (cf. concrete, formal).

logical: proceeding step by step in a manner which has been found to be the most efficient way of solving problems.

longitudinal: a *longitudinal* study is one carried out continuously on one child over a period. (cf. cross-sectional).

maladjusted: a *maladjusted* child is one whose behaviour is not acceptable and who seems to find it difficult to change it. (cf. adjusted).

maturation: the process of natural growth and development, as distinct from learning.

motivation: the processes which influence a person's behaviour.

need: a basic fundamental requirement or urge, either physical or psychological.

norm: an average or general standard obtained from observations of a large group.

perception: the whole process of both awareness and interpretation of information received through the sense organs.

personality: the sum total of the characteristics of a person as shown in his relationships with others.

potential: inborn possibilities, including those not yet shown or used.

regression: return to an earlier, less mature, level of behaviour.

reinforcement: strengthening, e.g. increasing the tendency to give correct responses by means of reward.

repression: preventing the free expression of natural desires and interests.

rote-learning: learning by pure repetition, regardless of meaning.

sentiment: feeling experienced regarding a particular person, object, or idea.

stimulus: any object or event which makes an impression on one of the senses, probably producing a response.

streaming: dividing the pupils in any year into forms or classes according to ability.

submissive: tending to accept other people's authority and direction. (cf. aggressive).

tactile: concerned with, or obtained by the sense of touch. (cf. auditory, visual).

tantrums: behaviour vigorously expressive of ill-temper, such as screaming or stamping.

temperament: the aspect of personality or make-up concerned with mood or level of energy.

visual: concerned with the sense of sight. (cf. auditory, tactile).

withdrawal: although he may not actually remove himself, a person may cease to take part in social contacts and current activity, usually from insecurity, or a feeling of inadequacy; this behaviour is called **withdrawal.**

Index

Abilities, see Intelligence
    Special Abilities
Adjustment, 84f, 89f, 102
Adolescence, 26, 91
Adventure, 24f
Aggression, 89, 102
Attitudes, 27, 78, 102

Child Study, 14, 95, 99
Concepts, 53f, 102
  development of, 58, 59
  moral, 86
  number, 58, 59
Conscience, 88
Convergence, 92, 102
Culture, 83, 103

Development, influences on, 16, 21f, 83f
  Principles of, 14, 15
Divergence, 92, 97, 103

Frustration, 89, 103

Gestalt, 42, 103
Group influences, 79, 80

Habits, 27

Identification, 27f, 103
Imagery, 73, 103
Individual differences, 11f, 96
Intelligence, 73f, 104
Intelligence tests, 74f

Language, 52f
Learning,
  as bond formation, 35f, 41, 42
  field cognition theory of, 40, 41
  programmed, 46, 47, 50, 51
  rates of progress in, 44, 45
  readiness, 70f
  reinforcement of, by need reduction, 37, 38, 41
  rote-, 43, 105
  stimulus-response theory of, 36f

Maladjustment, 84f, 91, 104
Marks, 45, 46
Maturation, 68f, 104
Mental age, 75
Moral concepts, 86
Motivation, 77f, 104

Needs, 23f, 89, 90, 104
Norms, of behaviour and development, 84, 85, 95, 96, 104
Number concepts, 58, 59

Perception, 72, 73, 104
Personality, 83, 97, 104
Programmed learning, 46, 47, 50, 51

Readiness, 70f
Regression, 63, 90, 104

Reinforcement, 37, 38, 41, 105
Rewards, 45f

Security, 24f
Self, 87, 88
Special abilities and aptitudes, 76, 77
Studies of children, 14, 95, 99
  Cross-sectional, 14, 103
  Longitudinal, 14, 104

Theories in Psychology, 17, 18
Thinking, 59f
  concrete, 62, 63
  formal, 62, 63
  intuitive, 61, 63